Coloring Book For Adults
Science & Technology
Relaxation

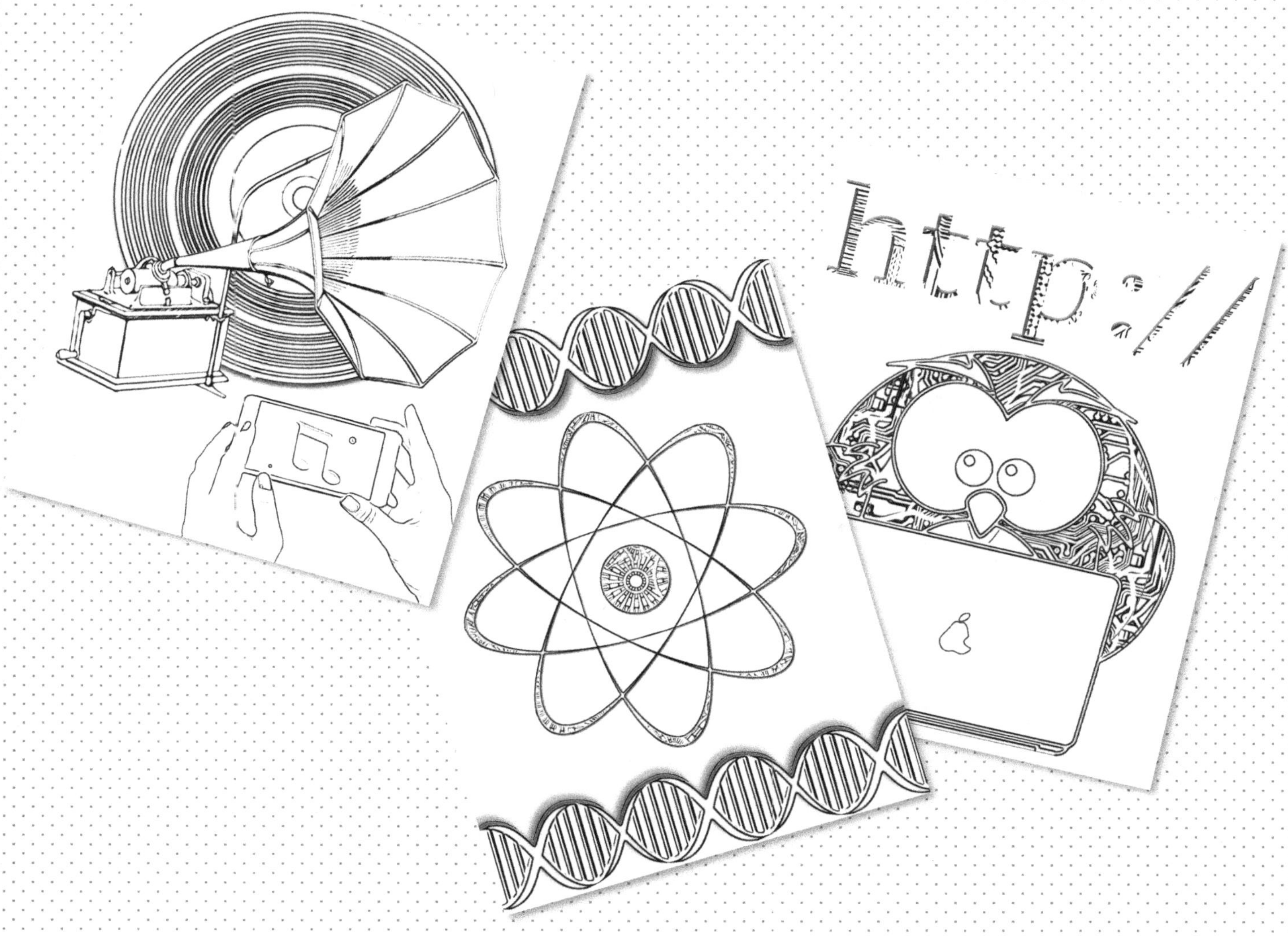

Images Beginner to Advanced

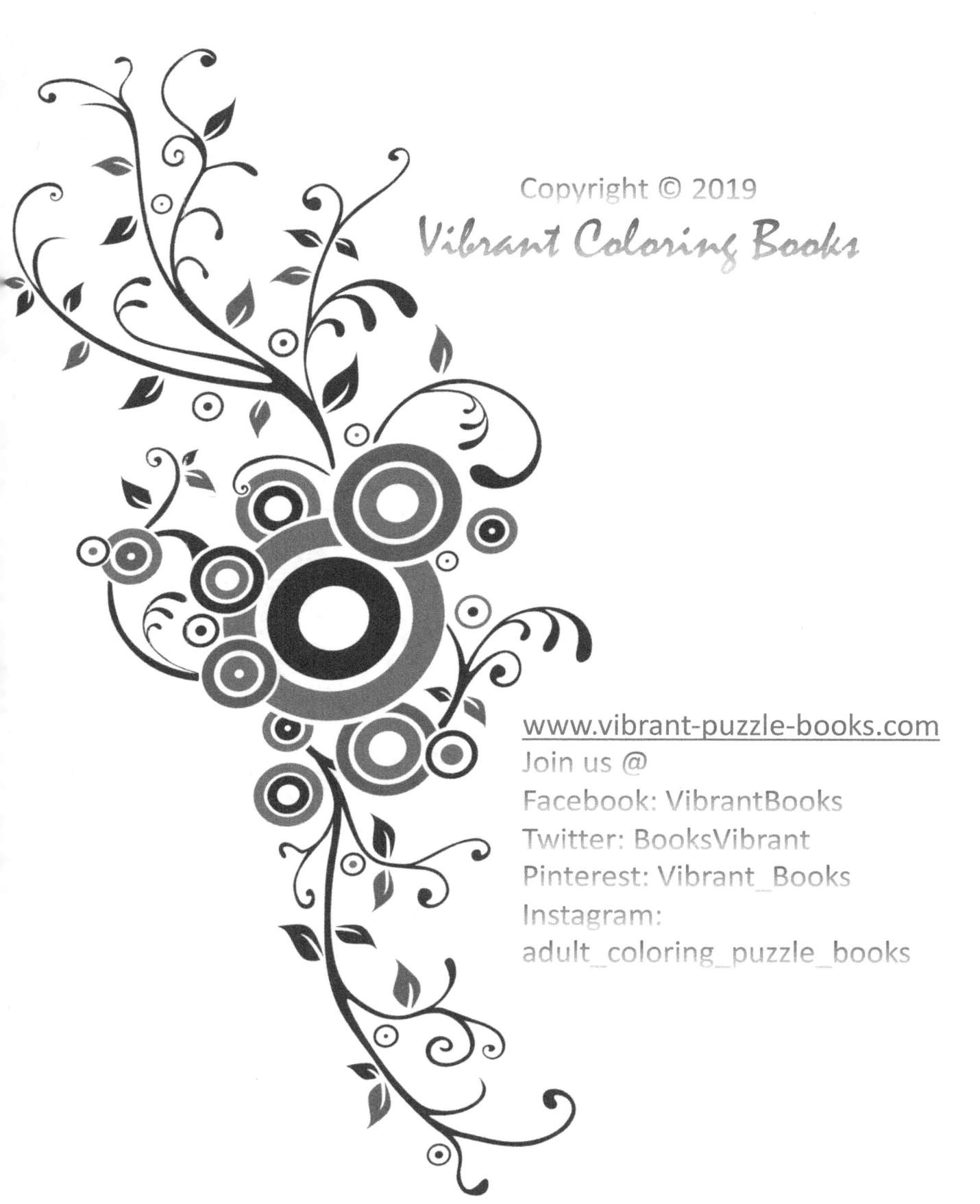

Copyright © 2019
Vibrant Coloring Books

www.vibrant-puzzle-books.com
Join us @
Facebook: VibrantBooks
Twitter: BooksVibrant
Pinterest: Vibrant_Books
Instagram:
adult_coloring_puzzle_books

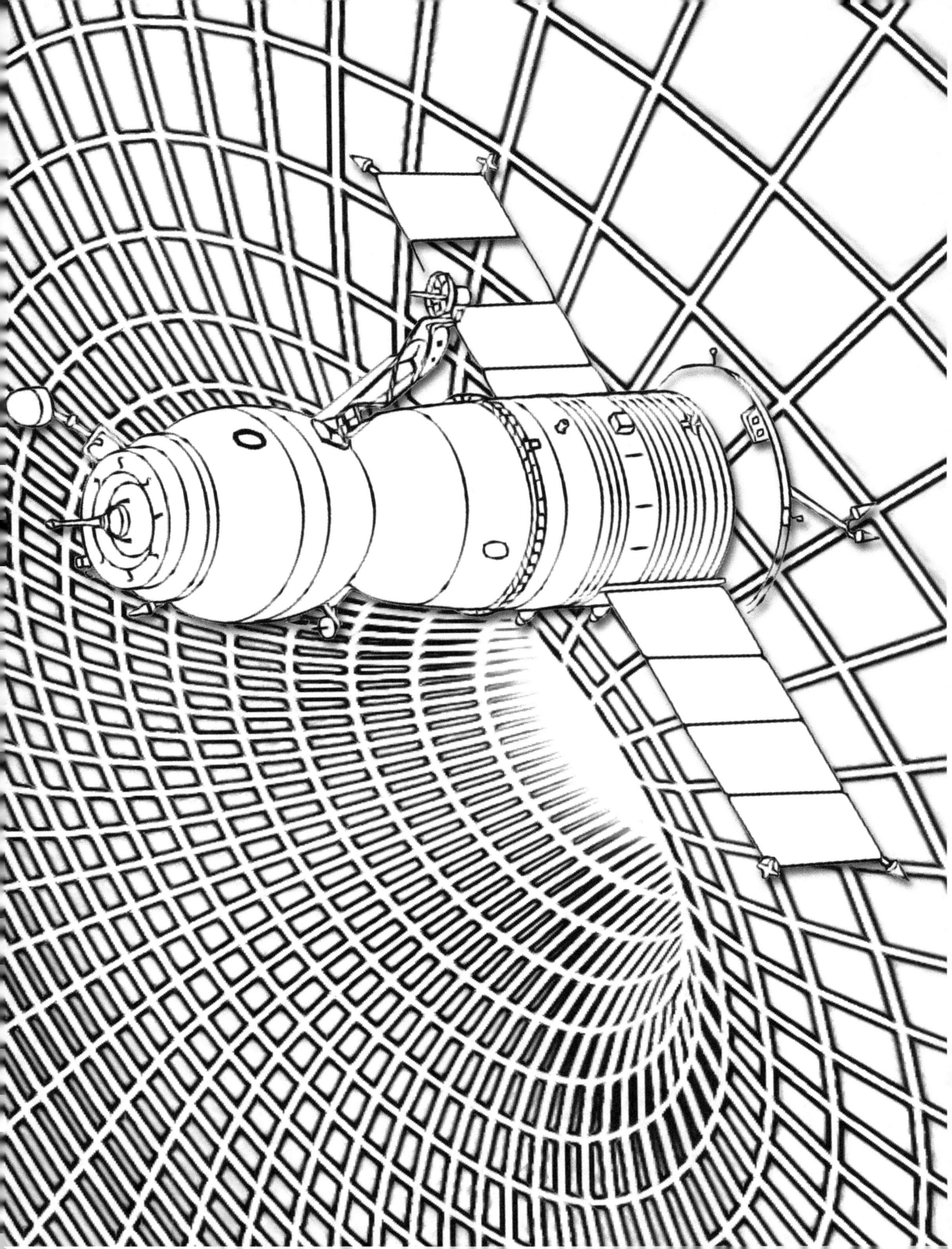

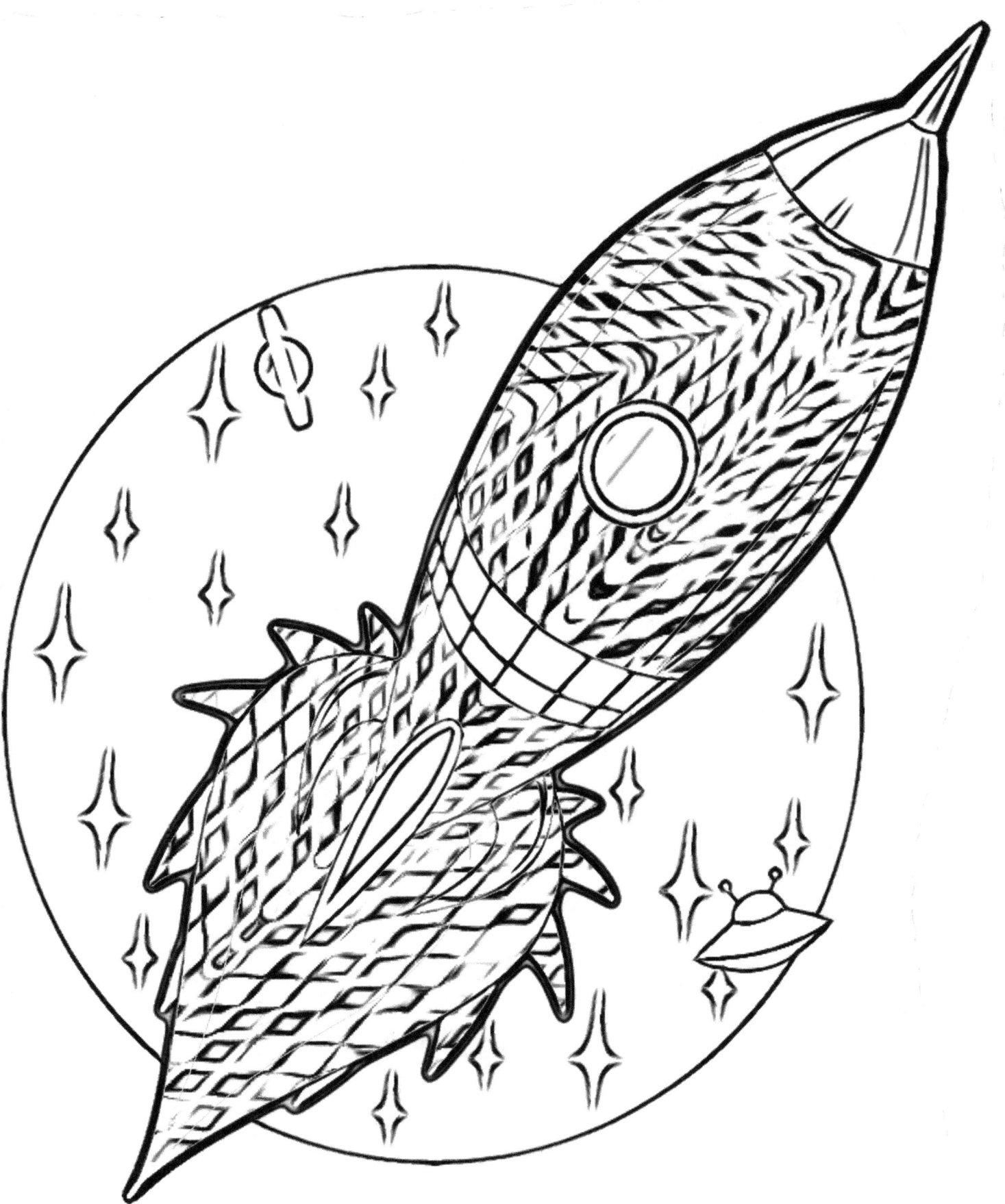

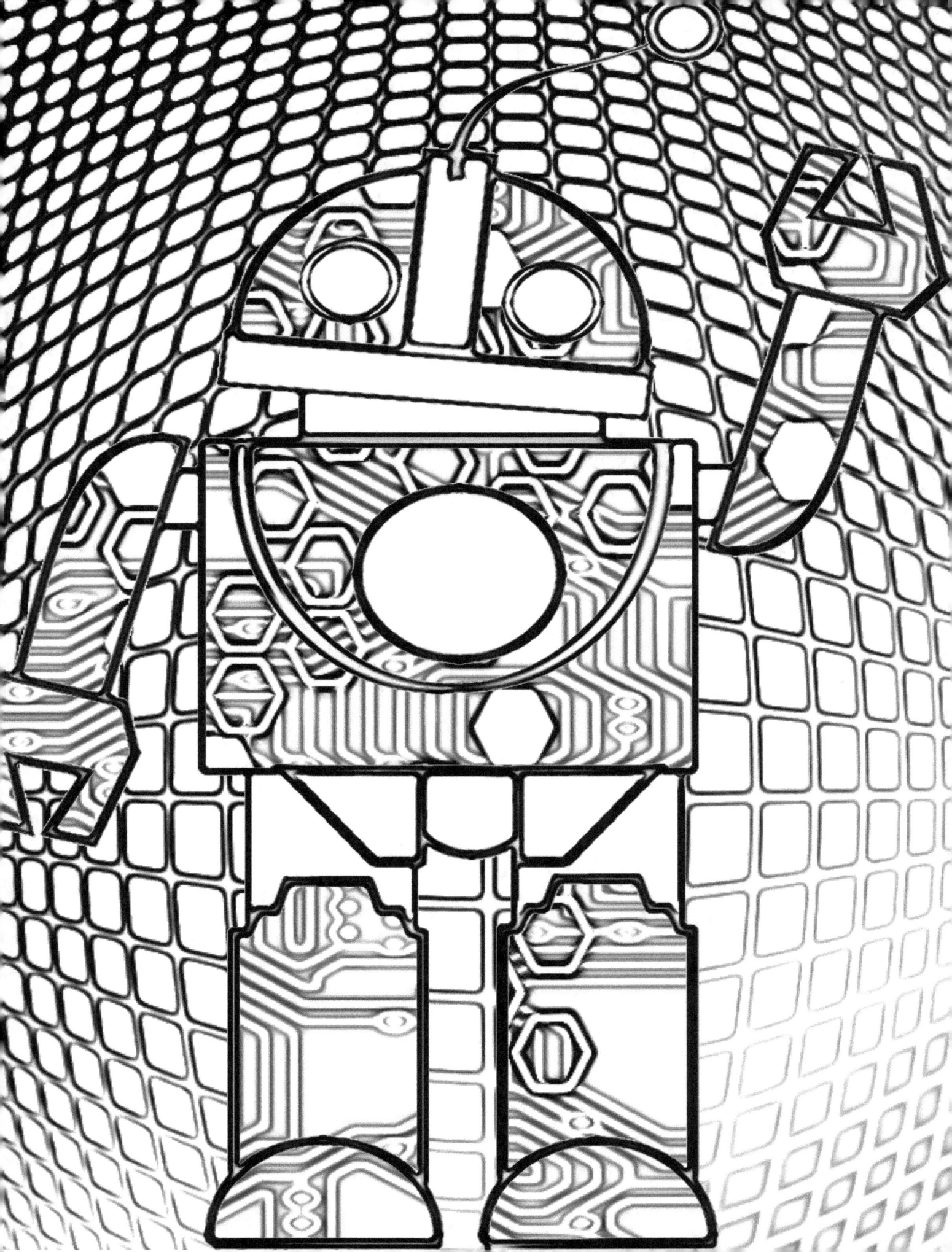

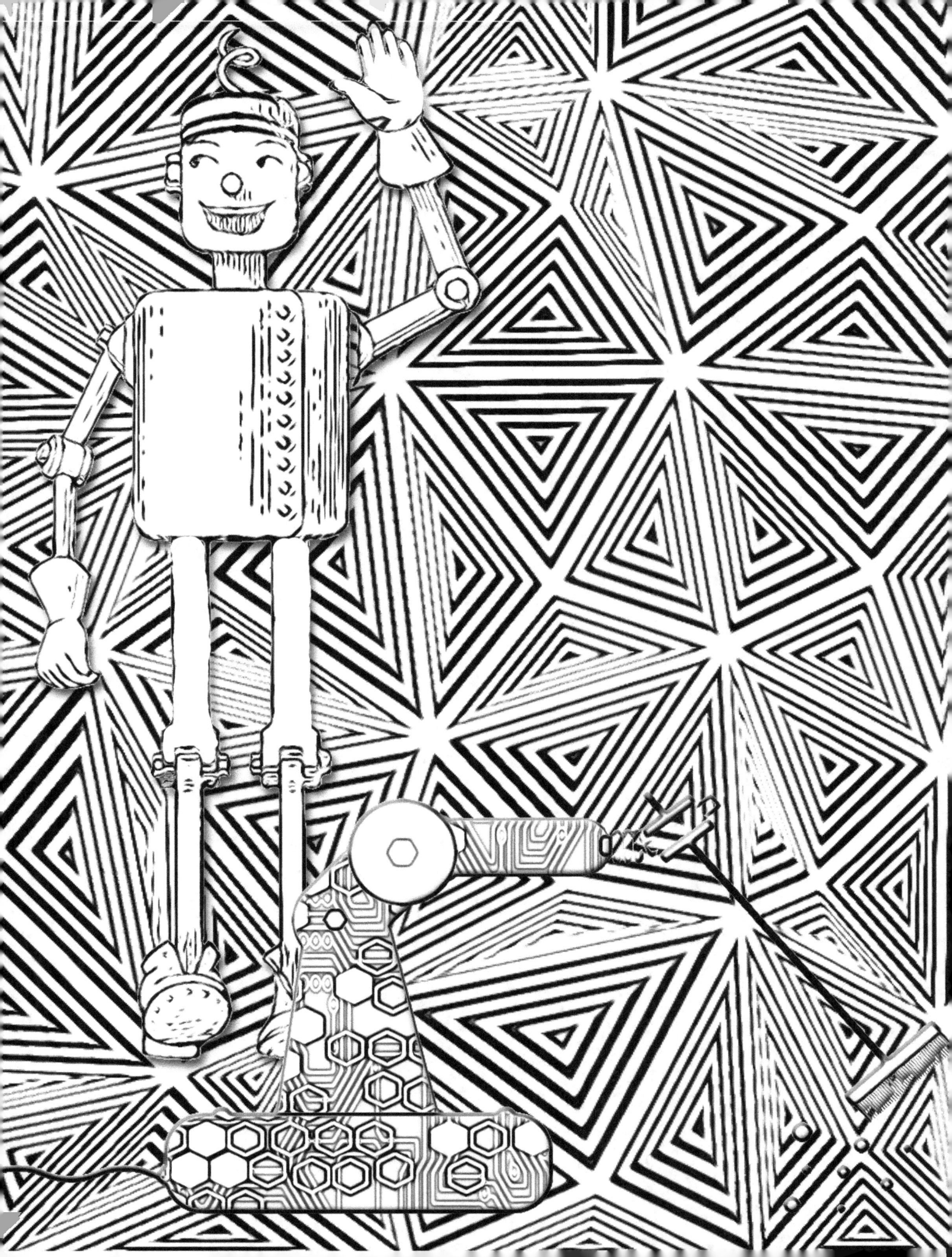

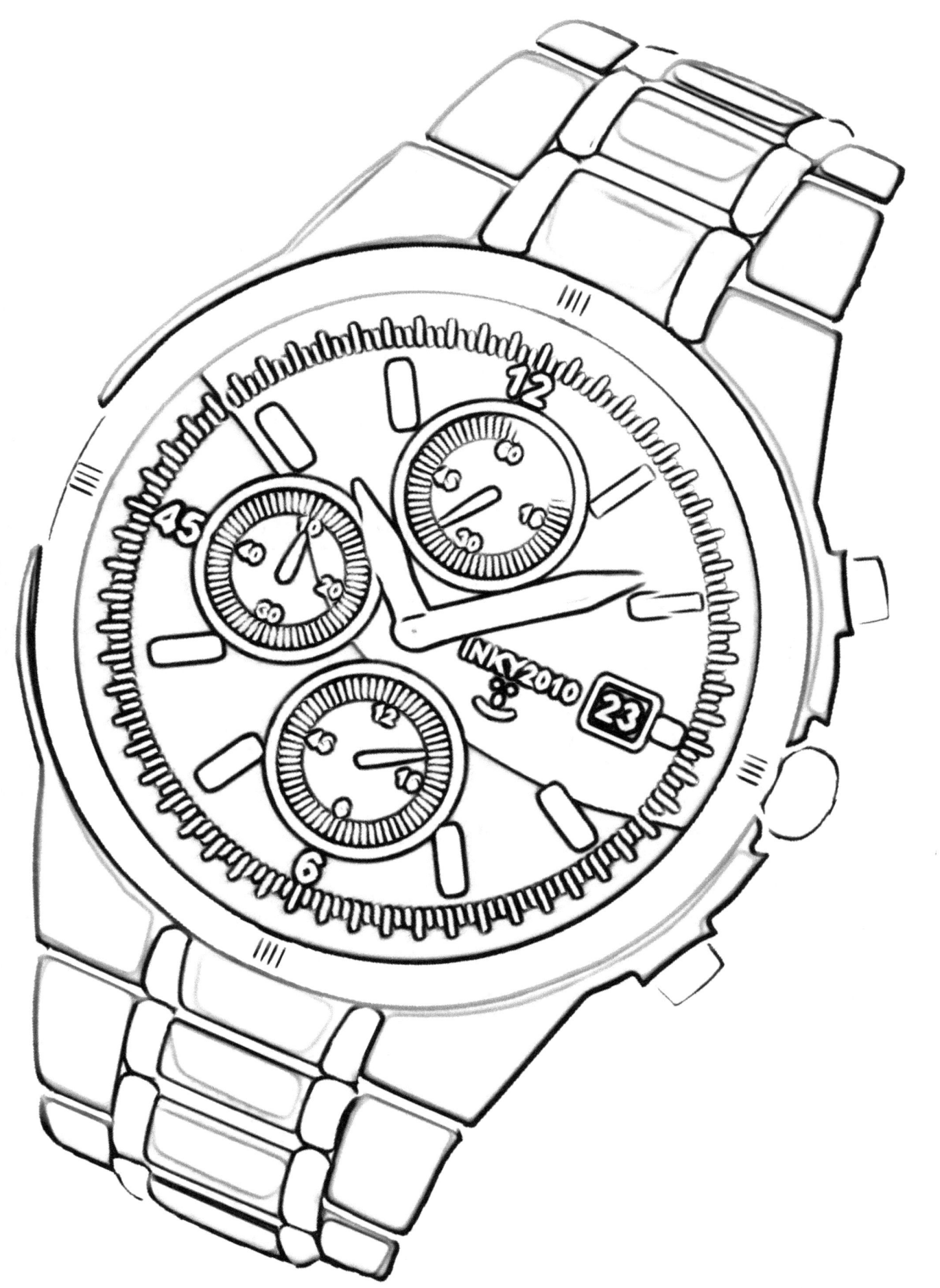

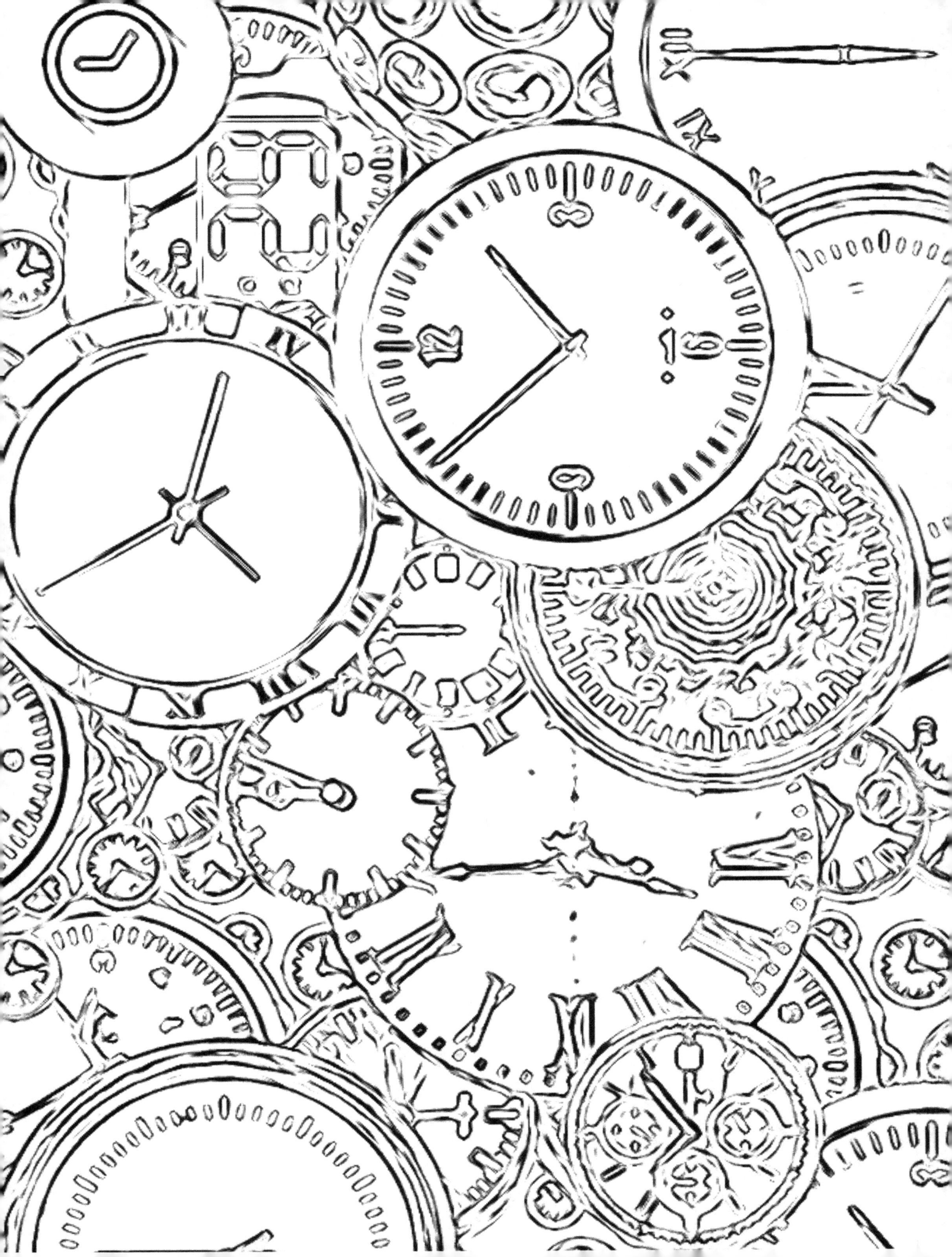

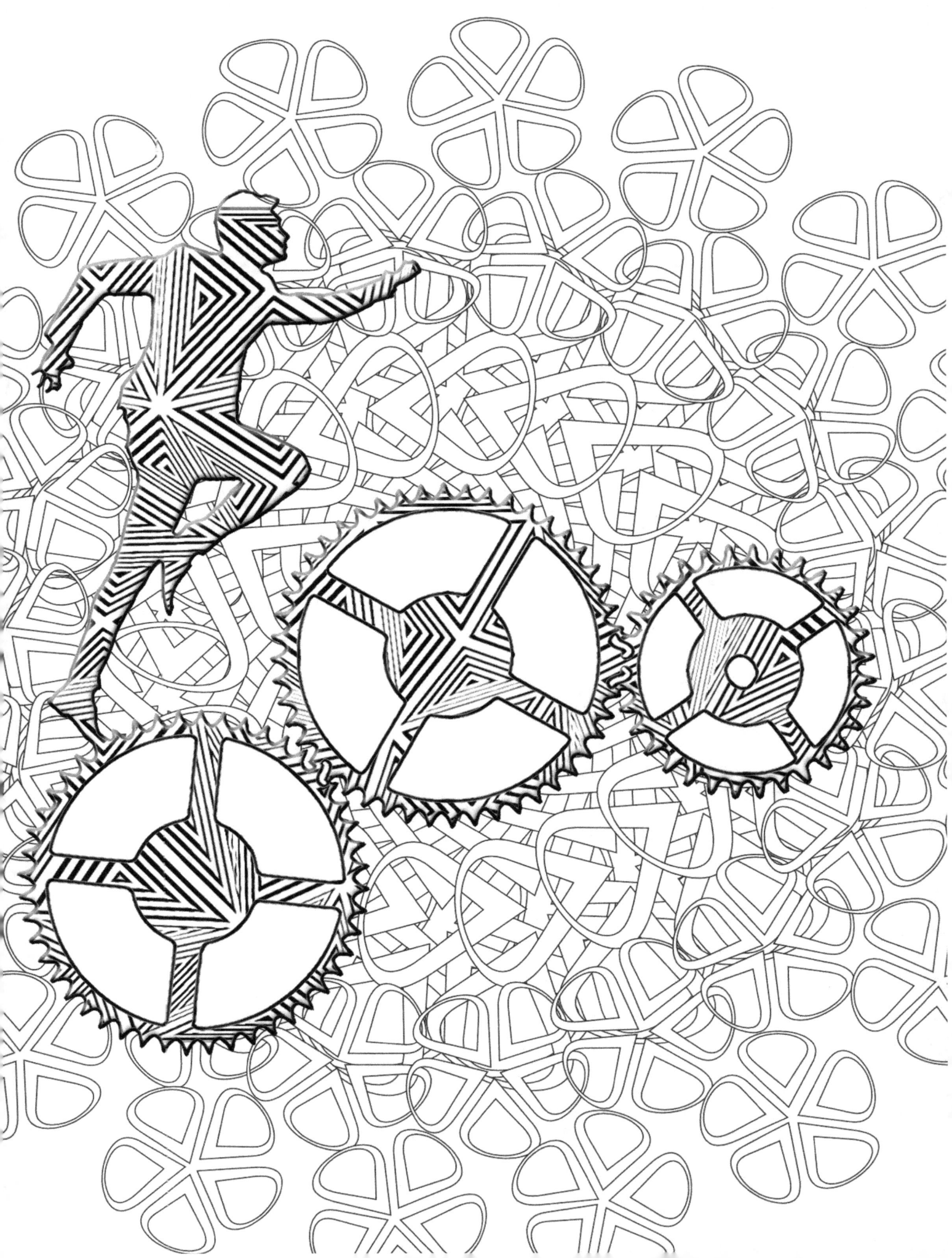

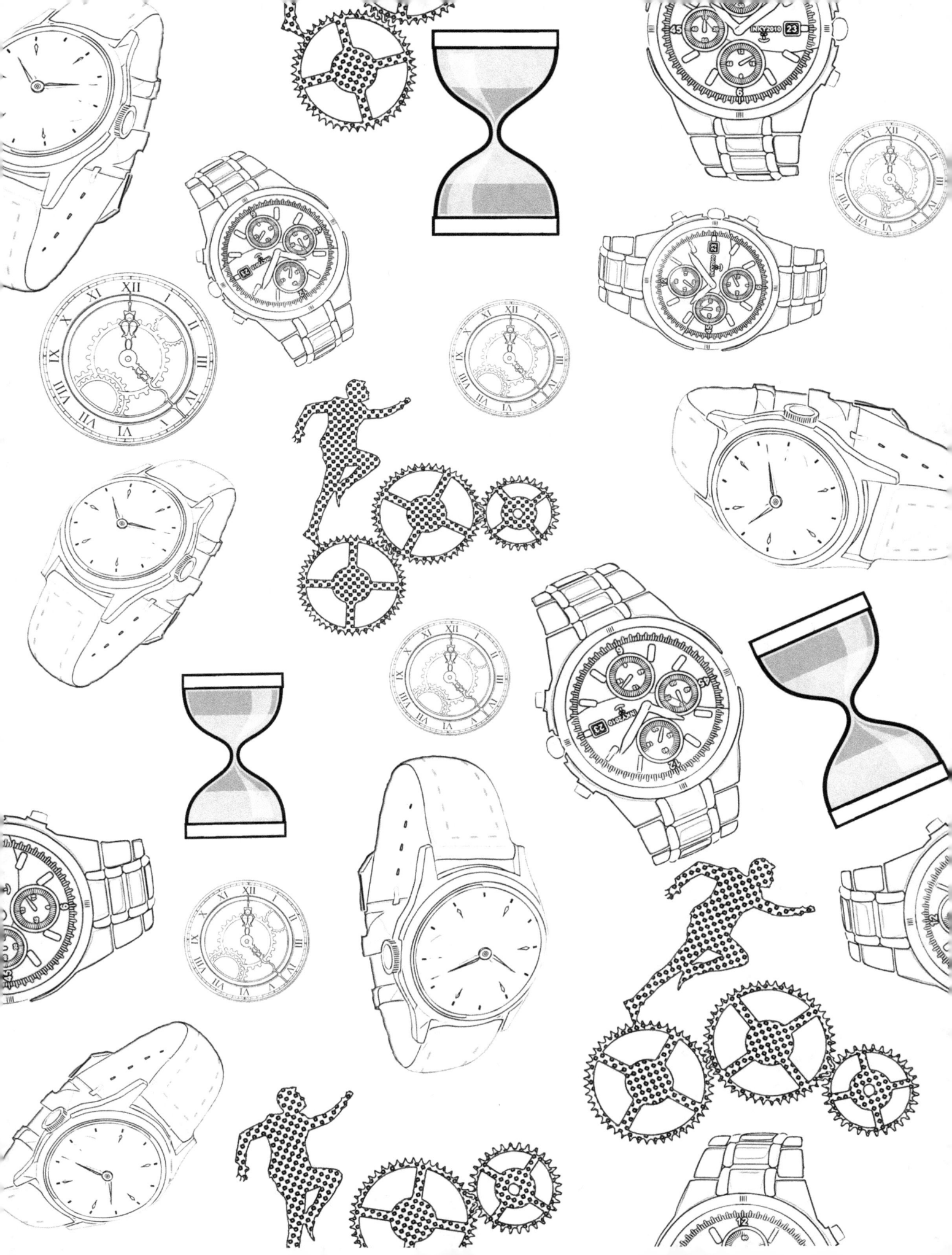

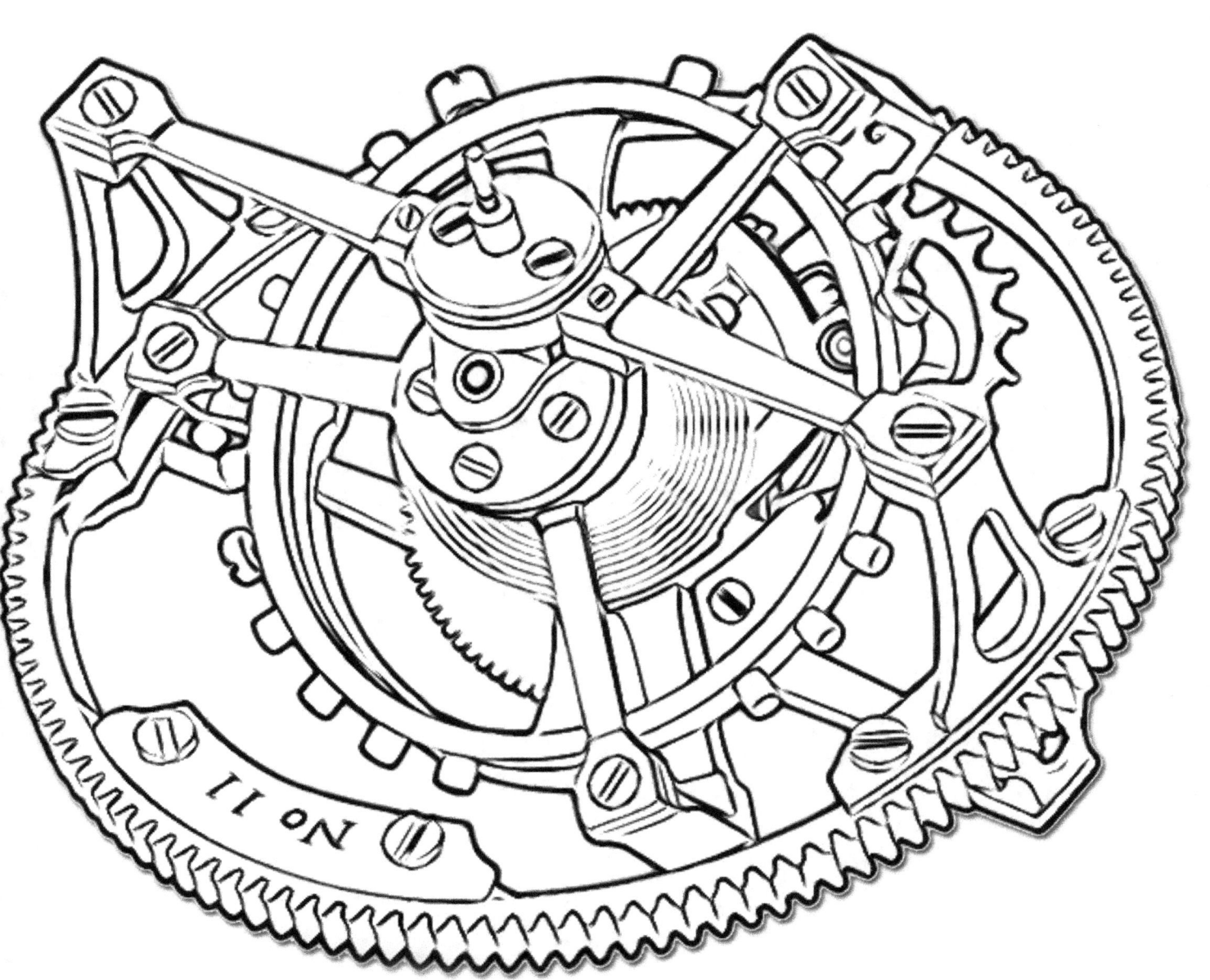

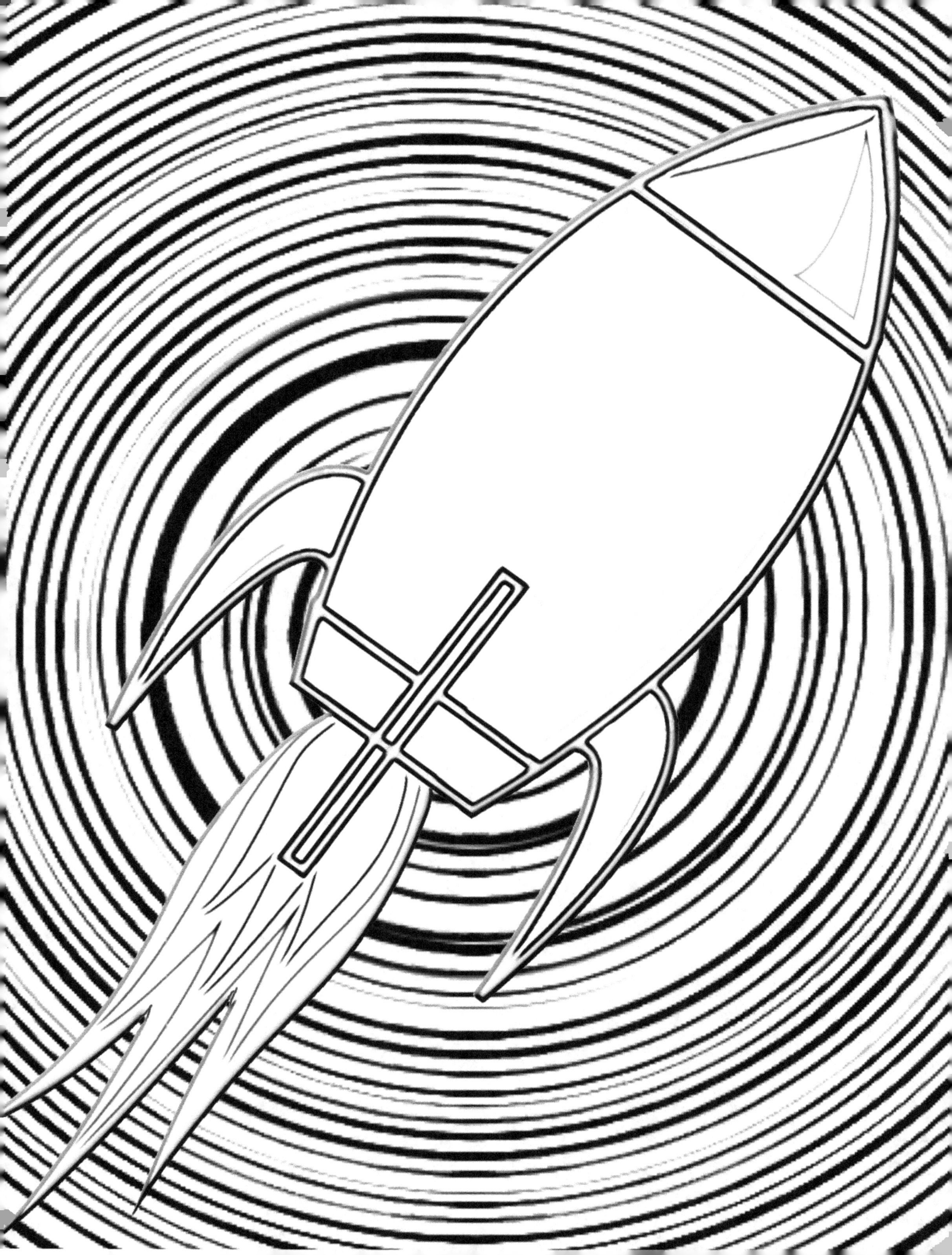

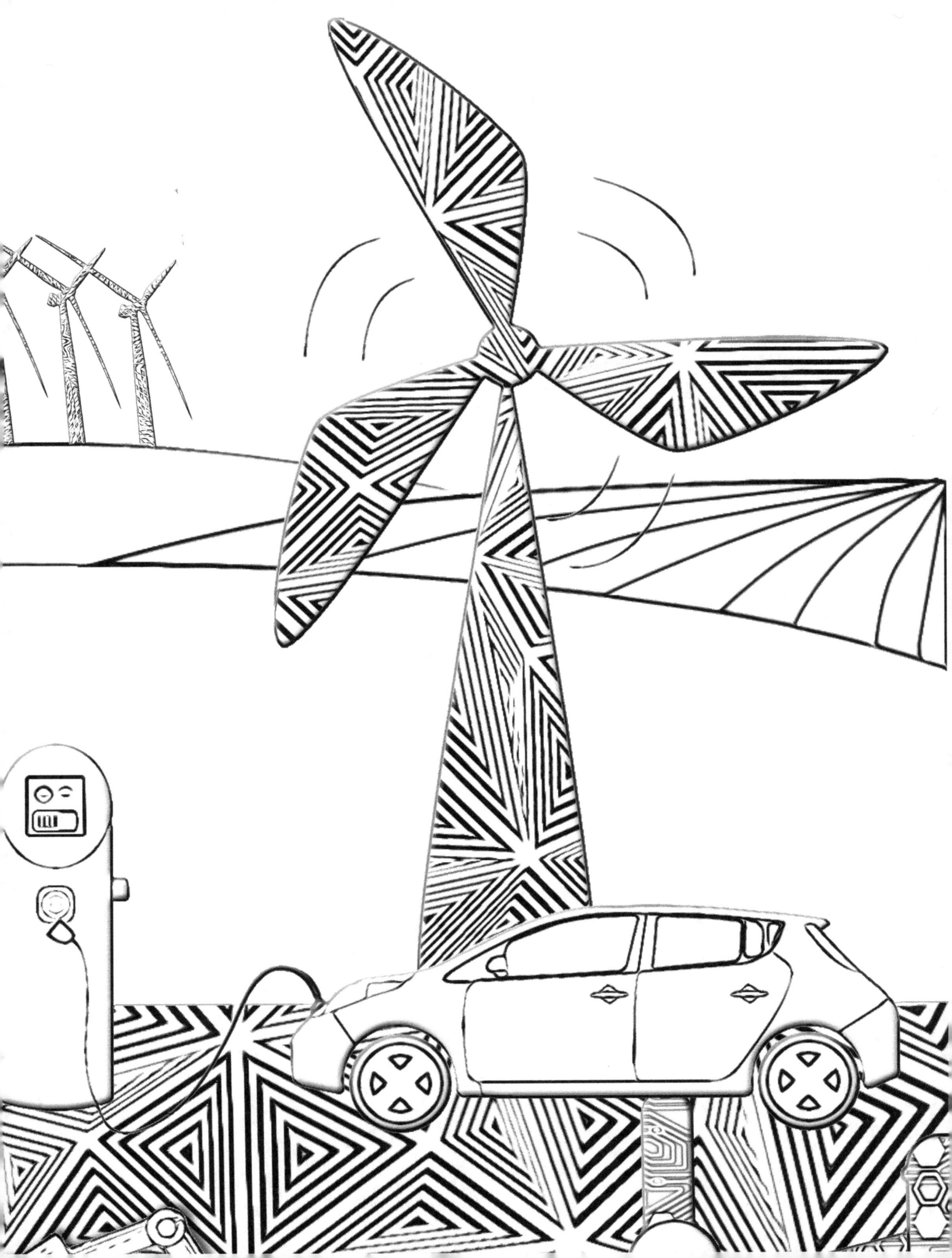

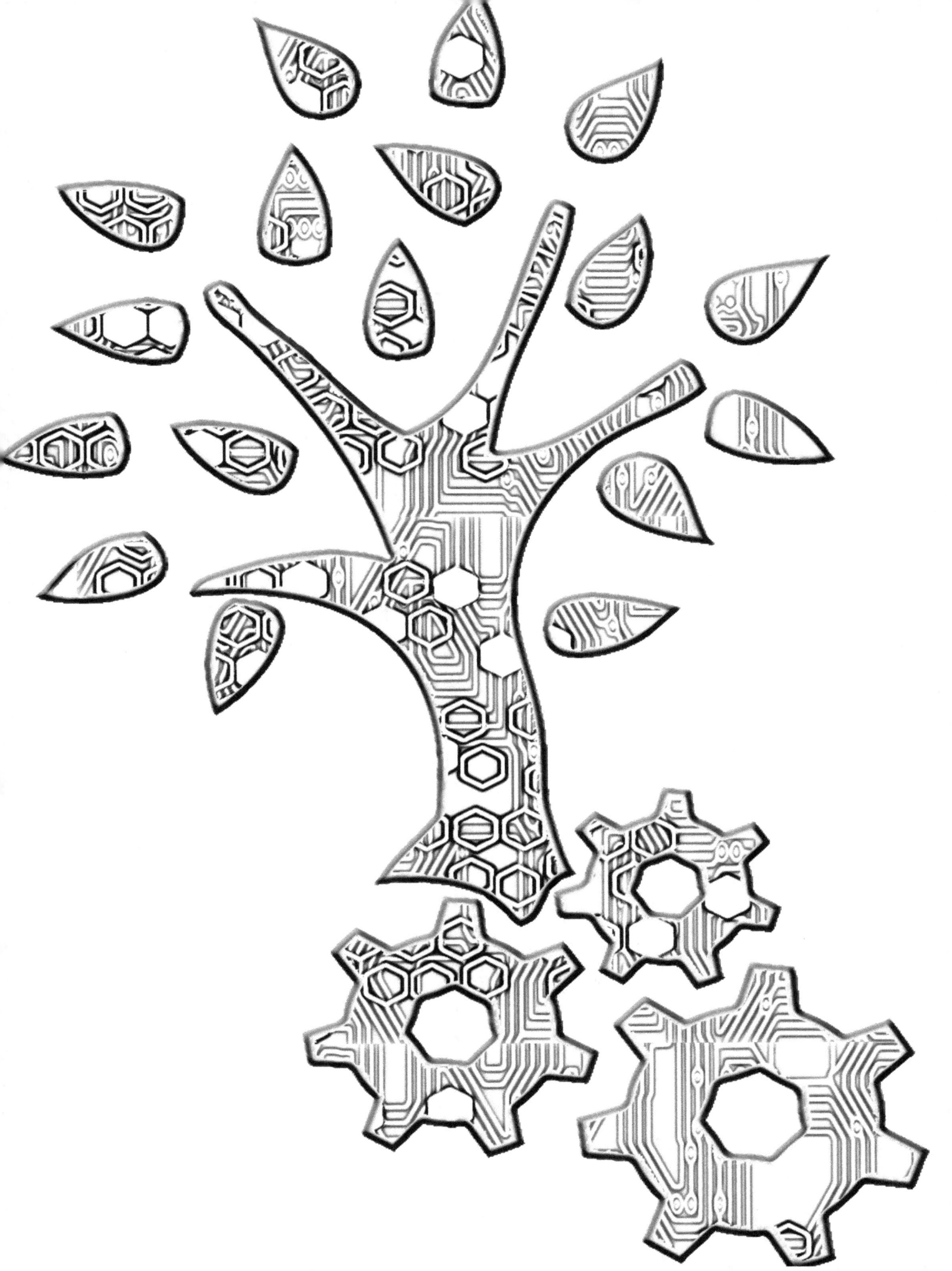

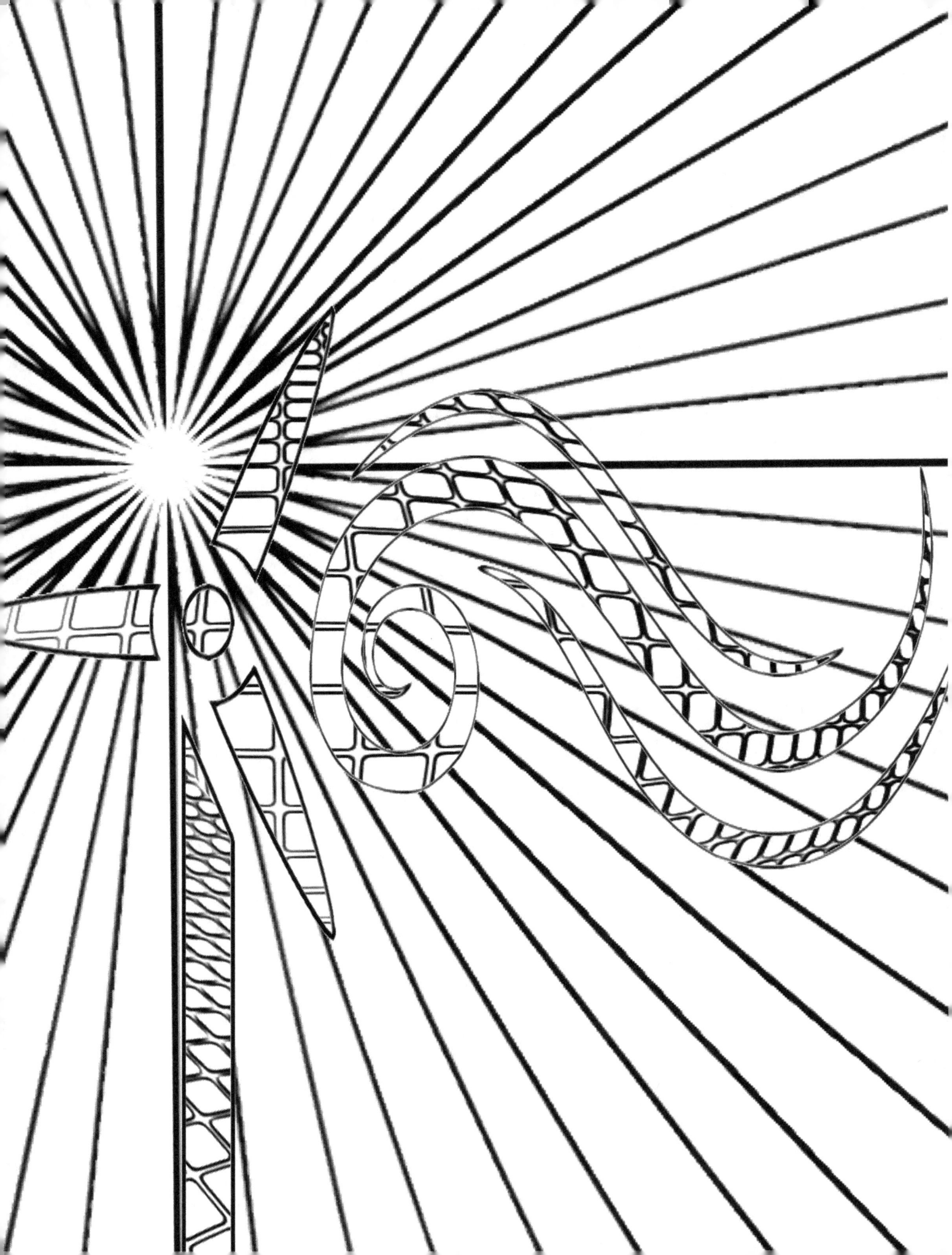

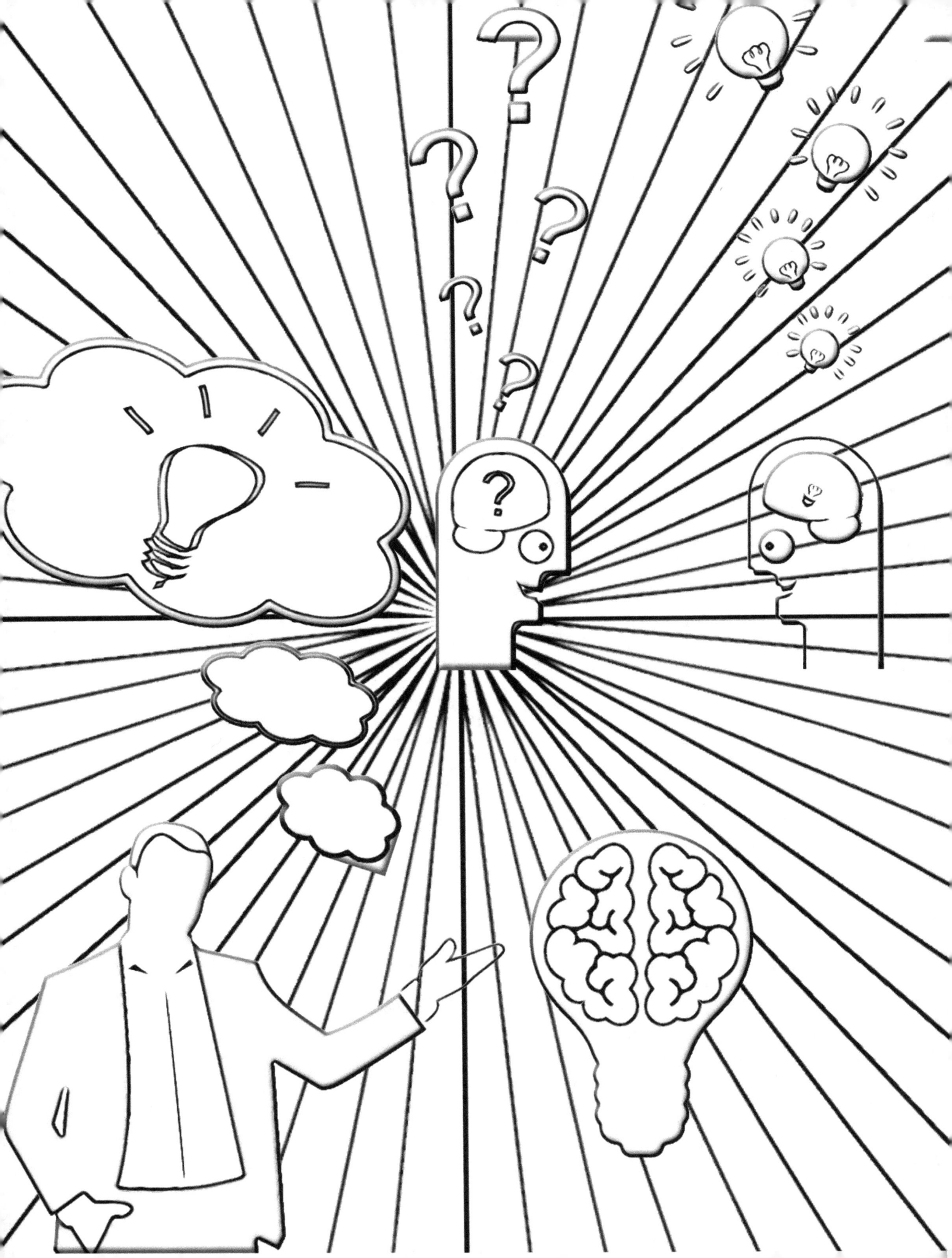

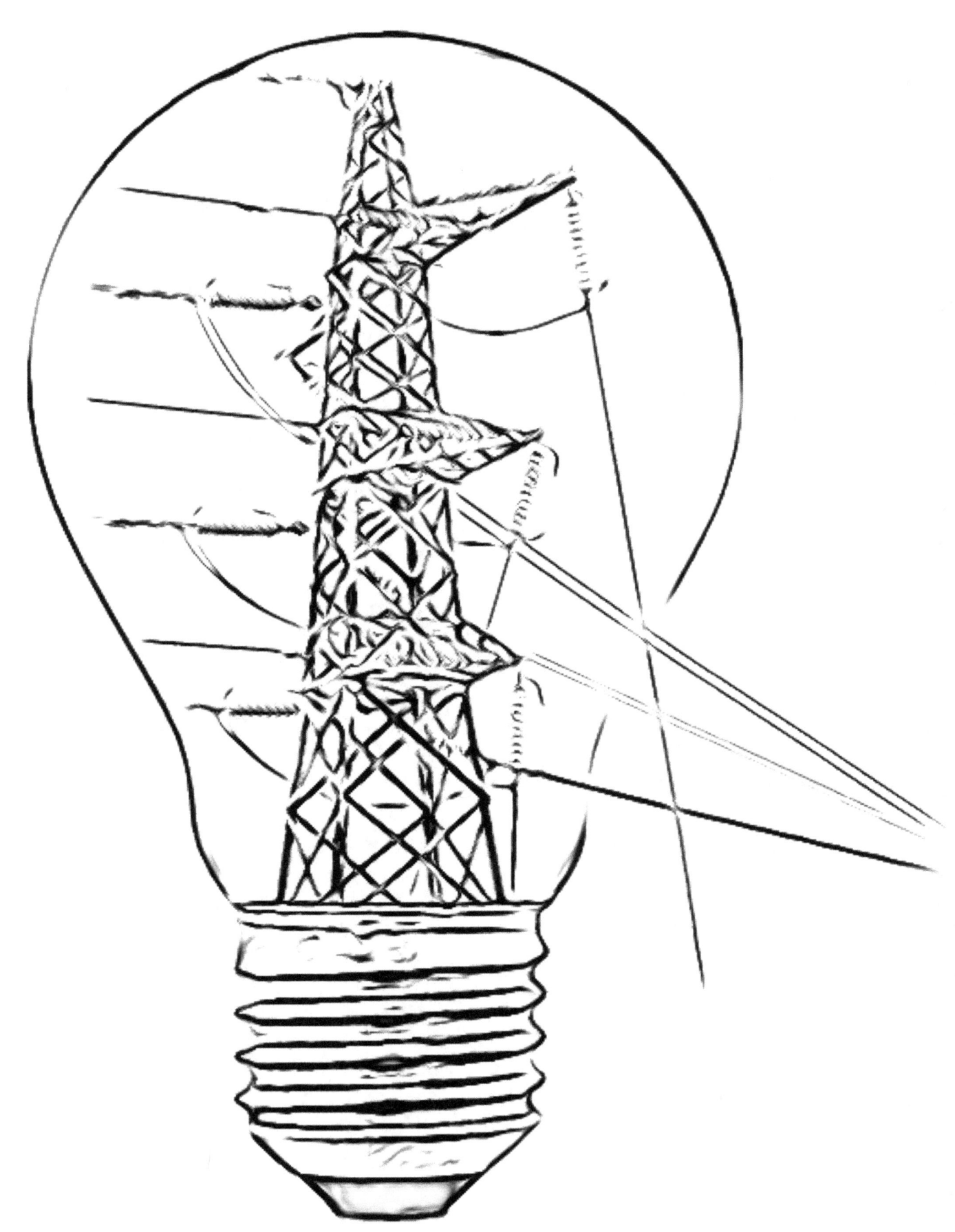

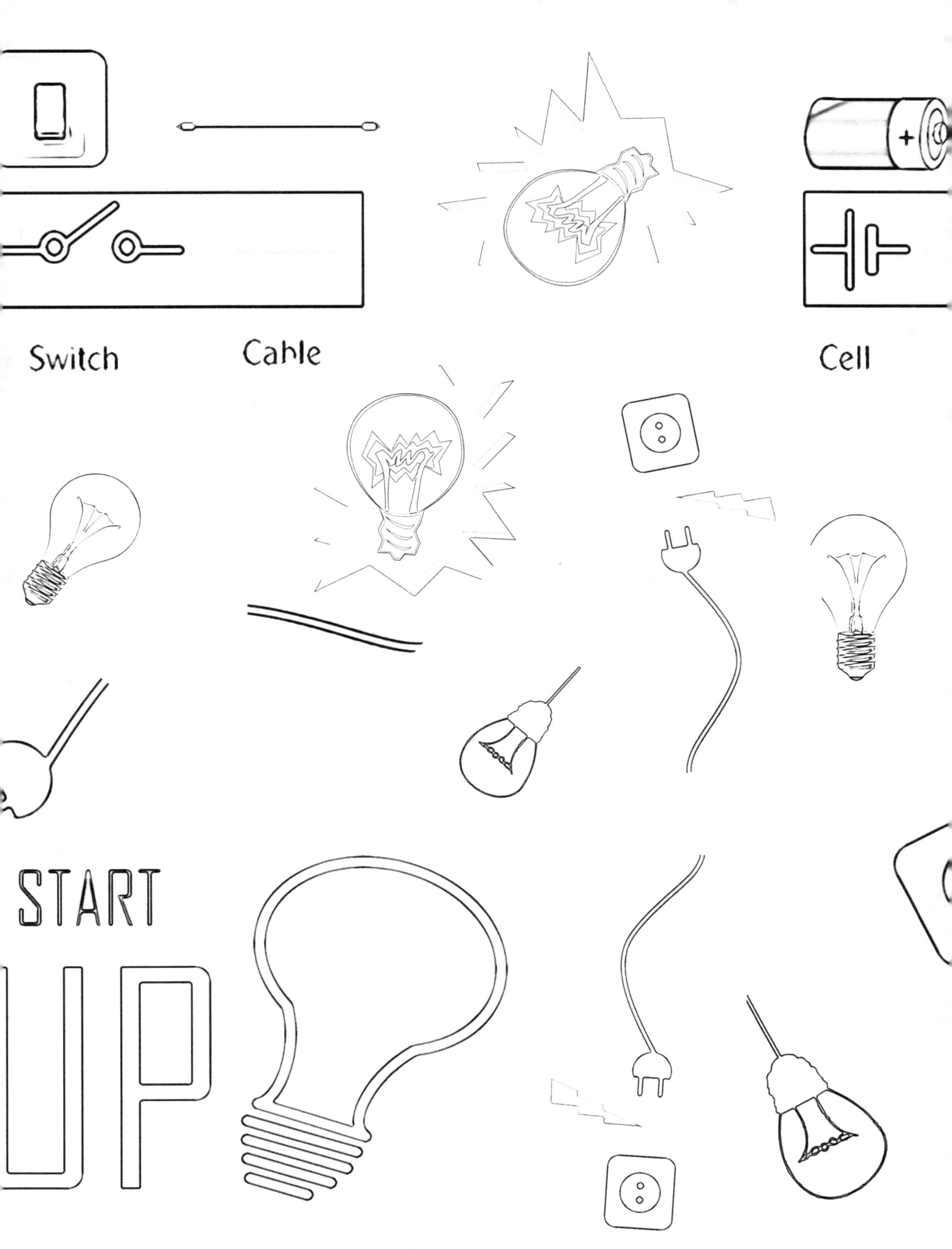

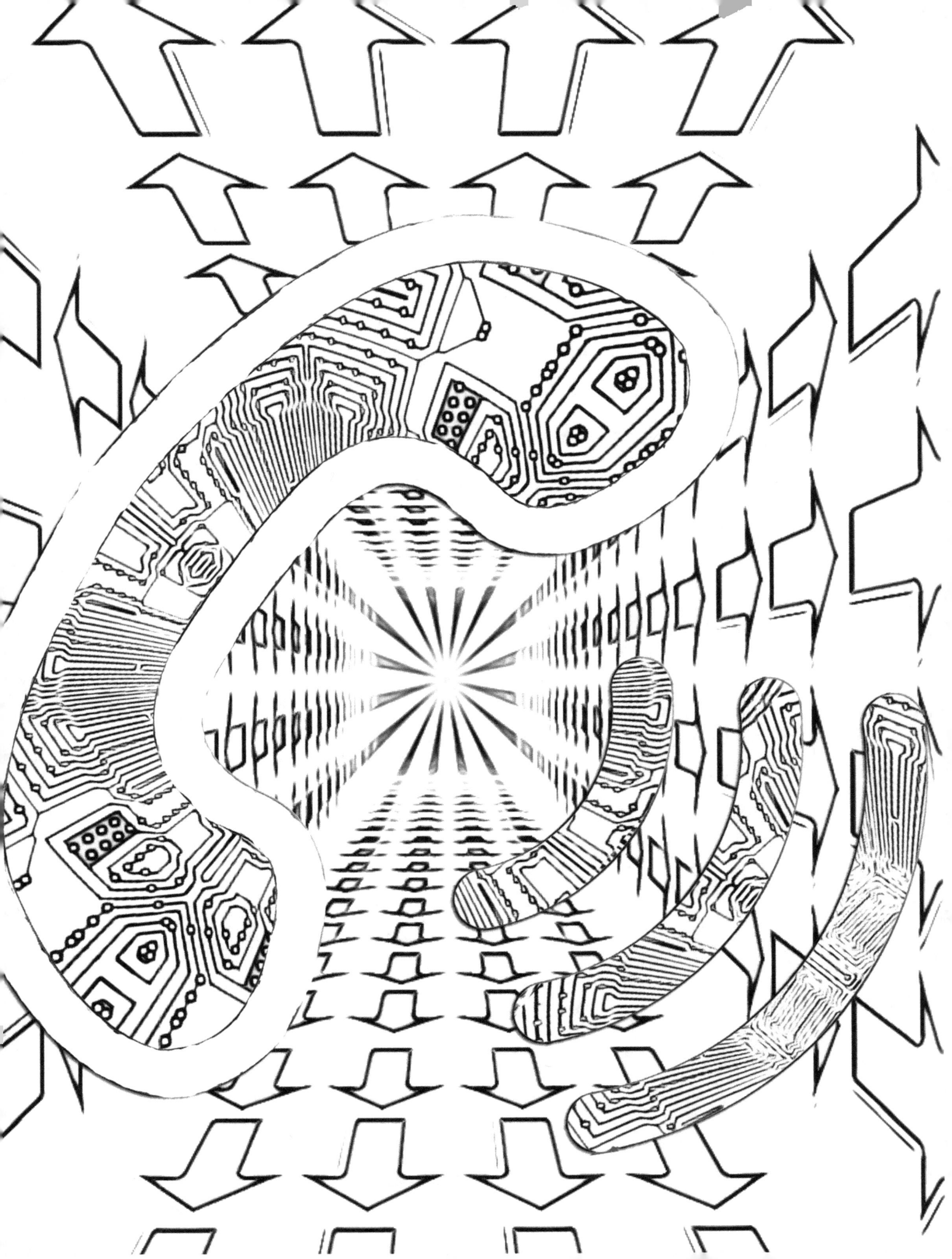

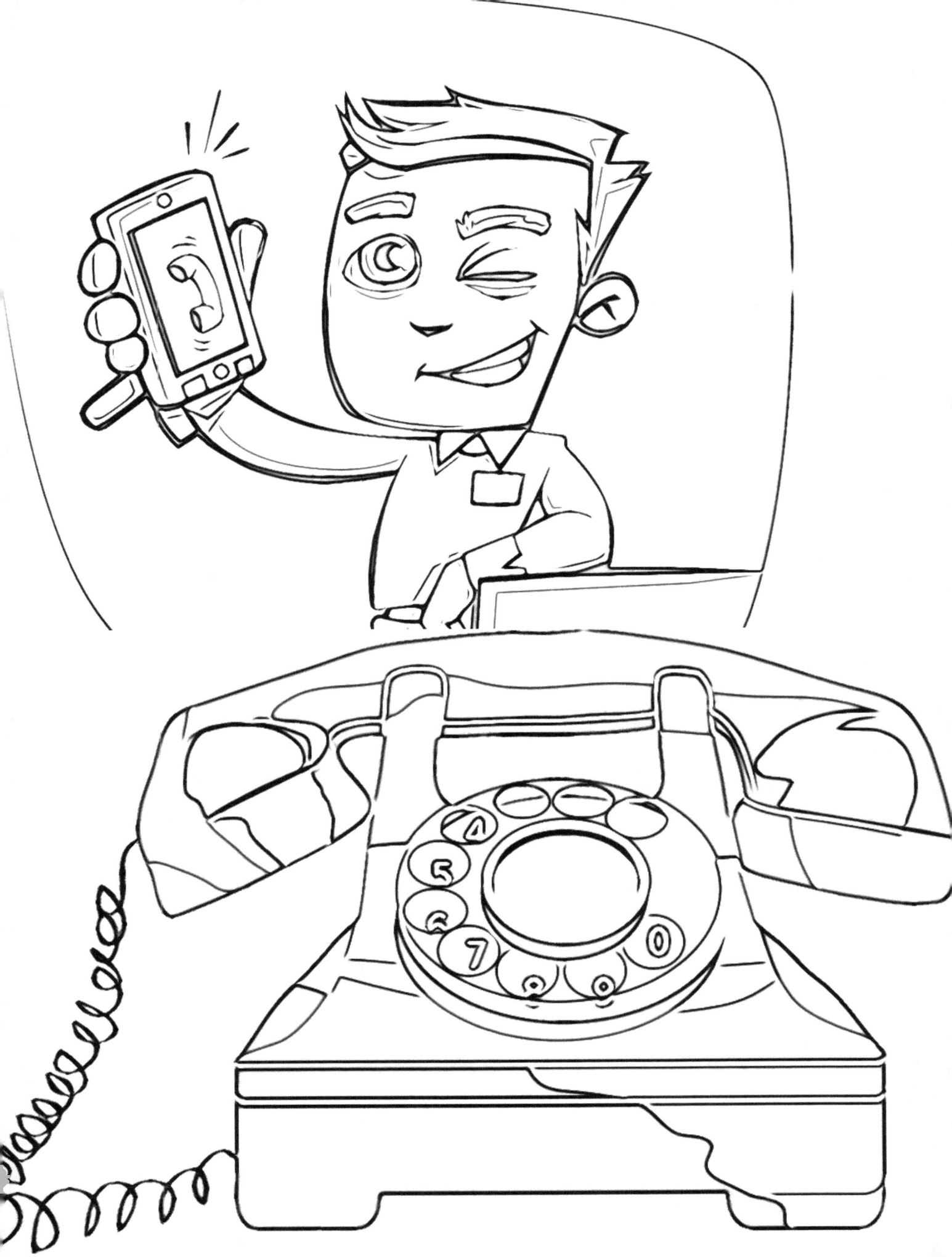

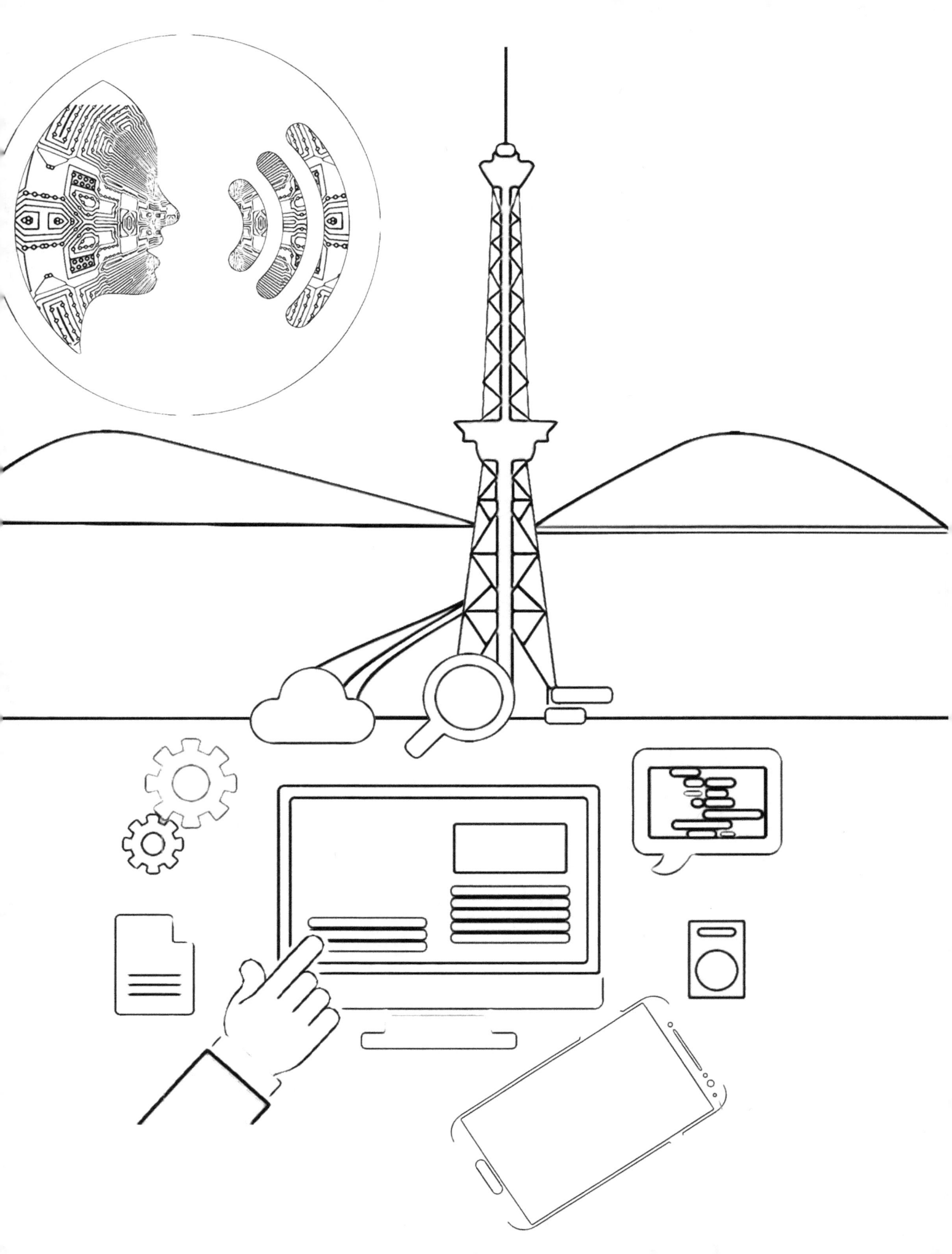

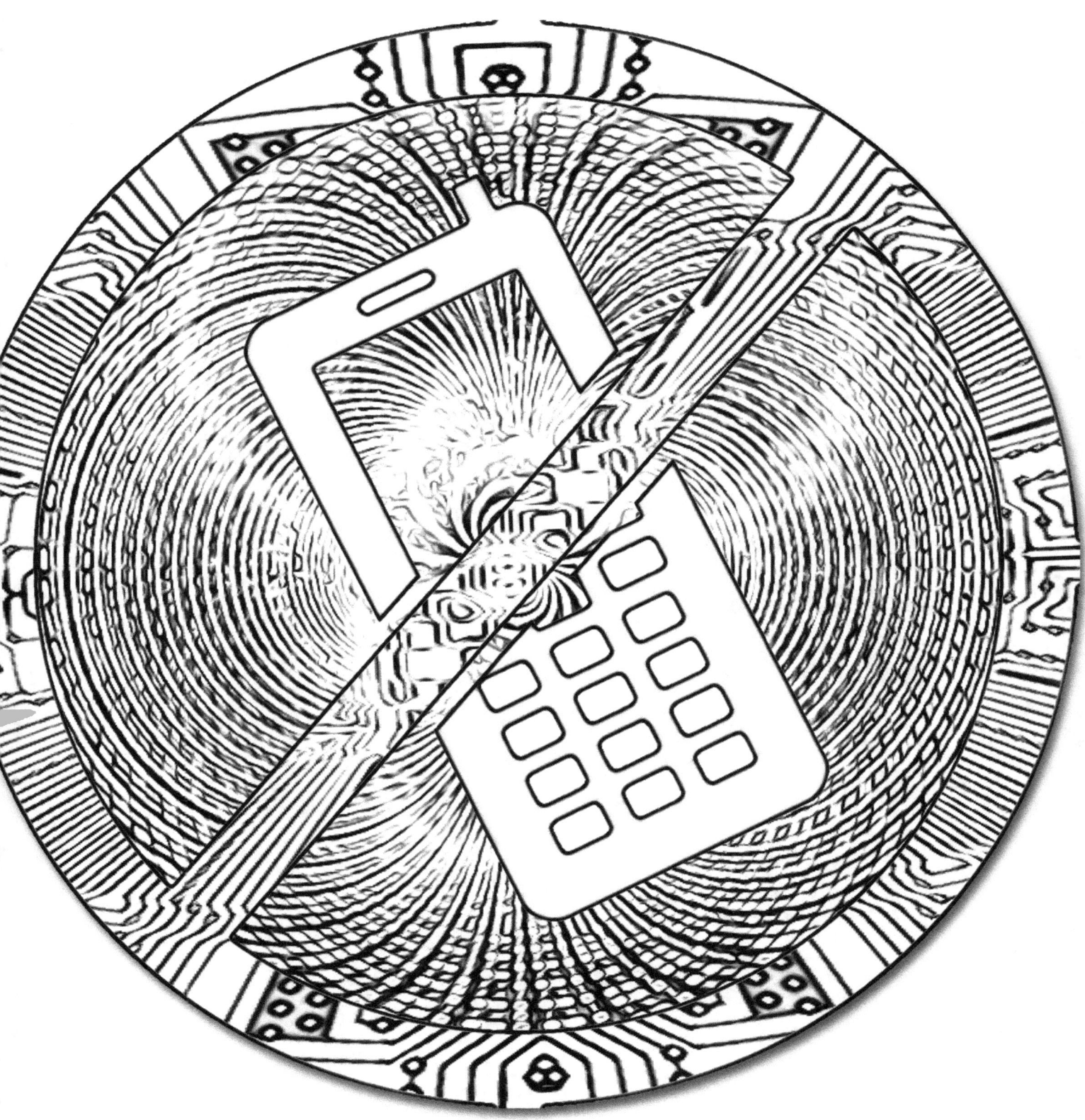

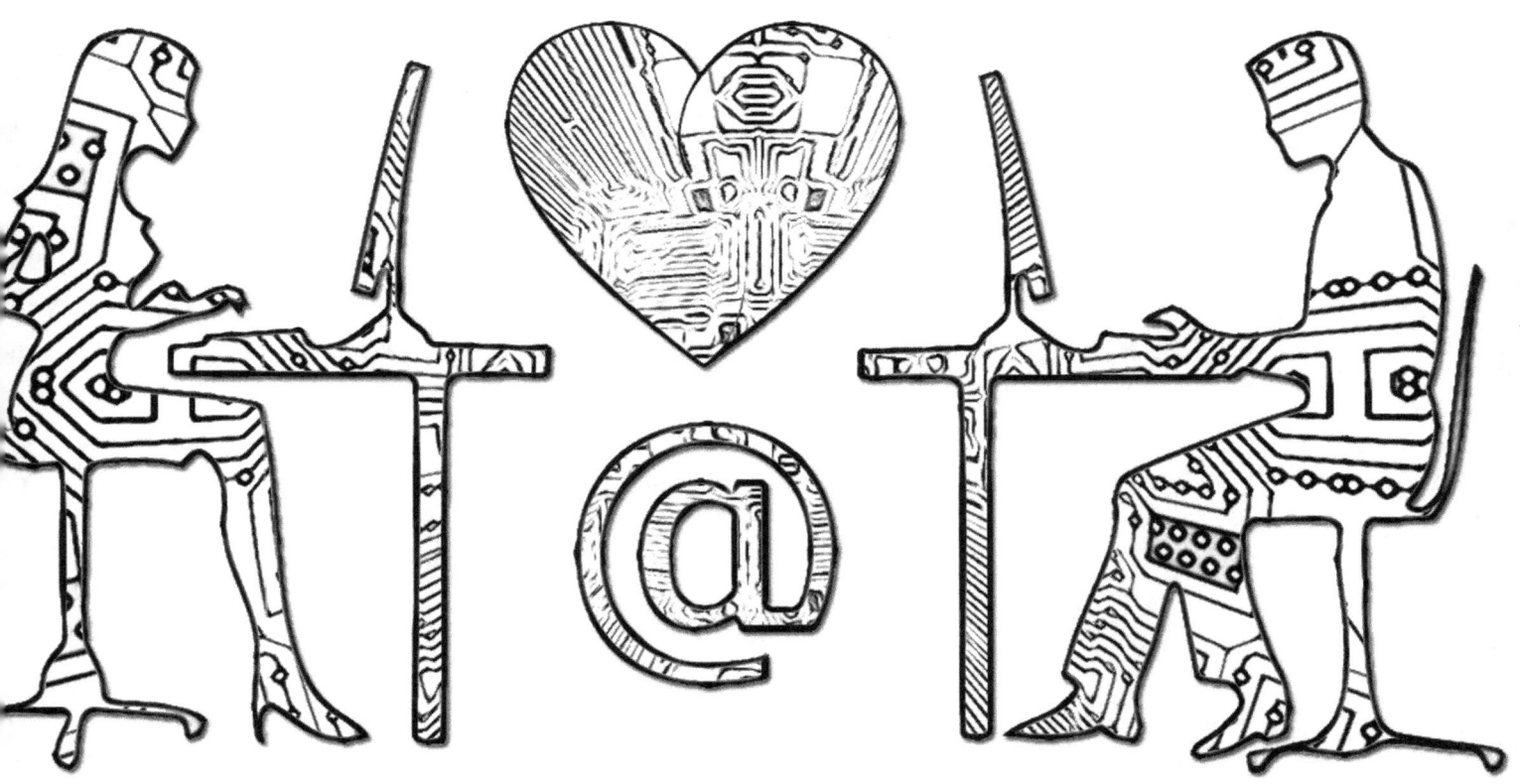

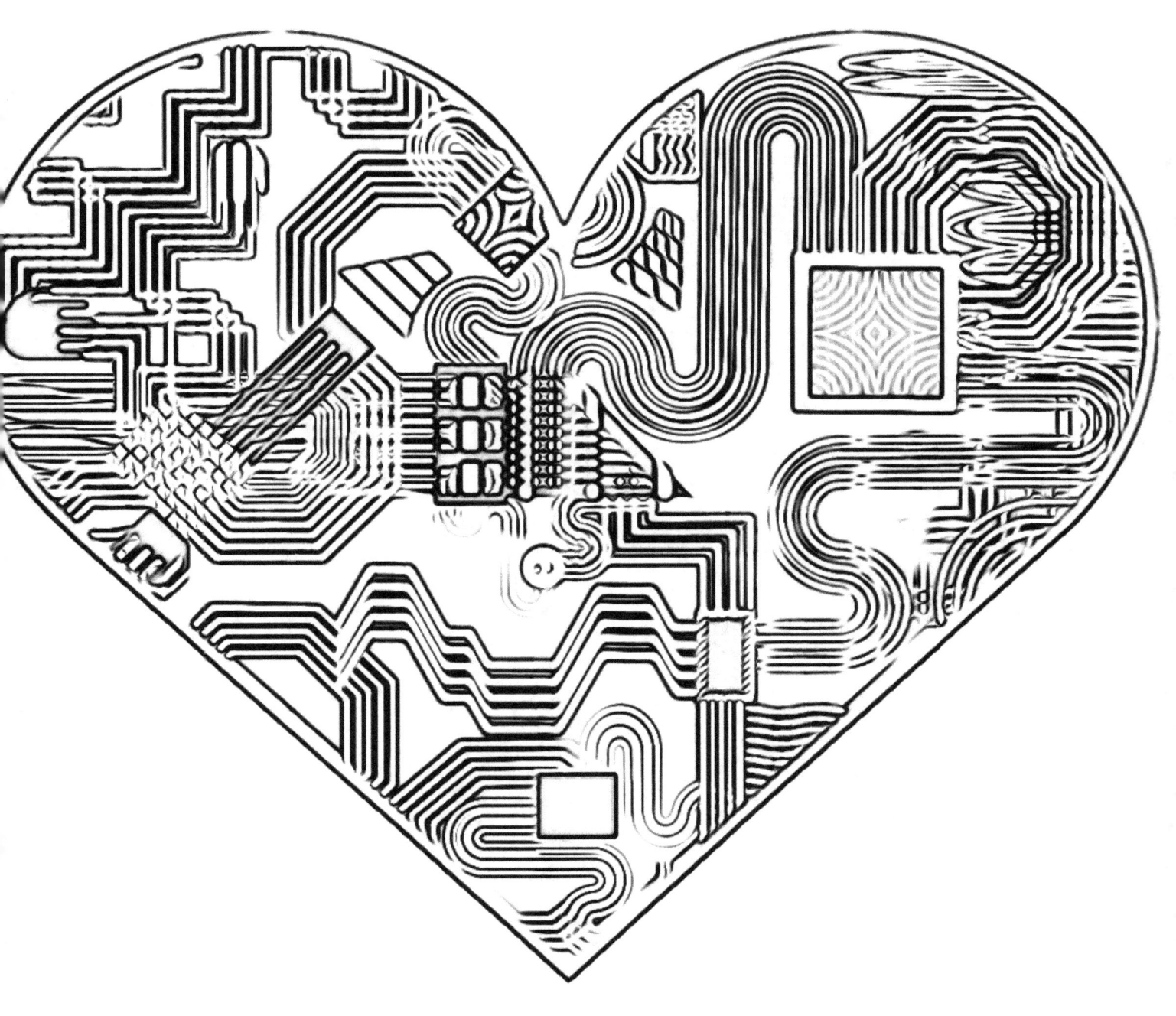

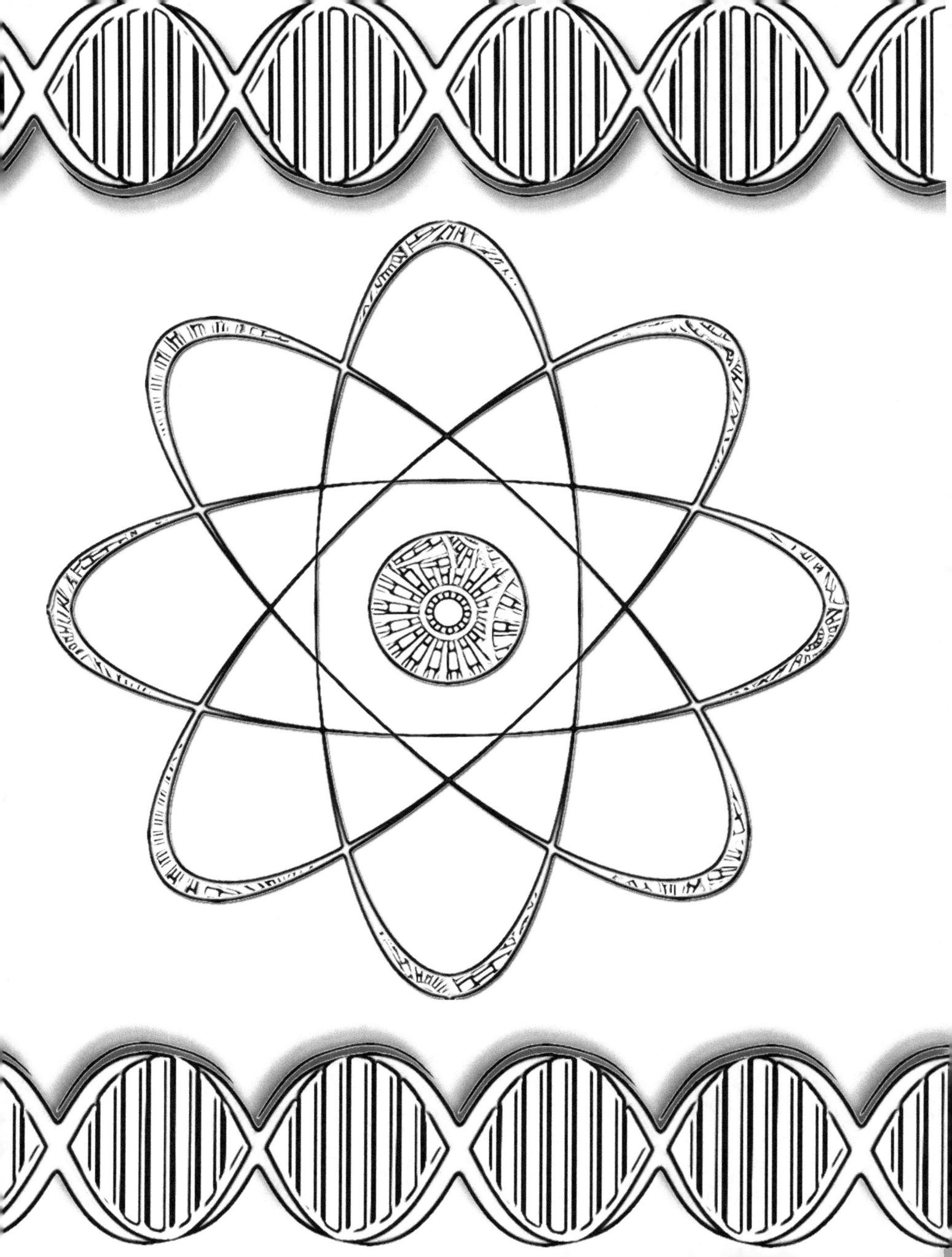

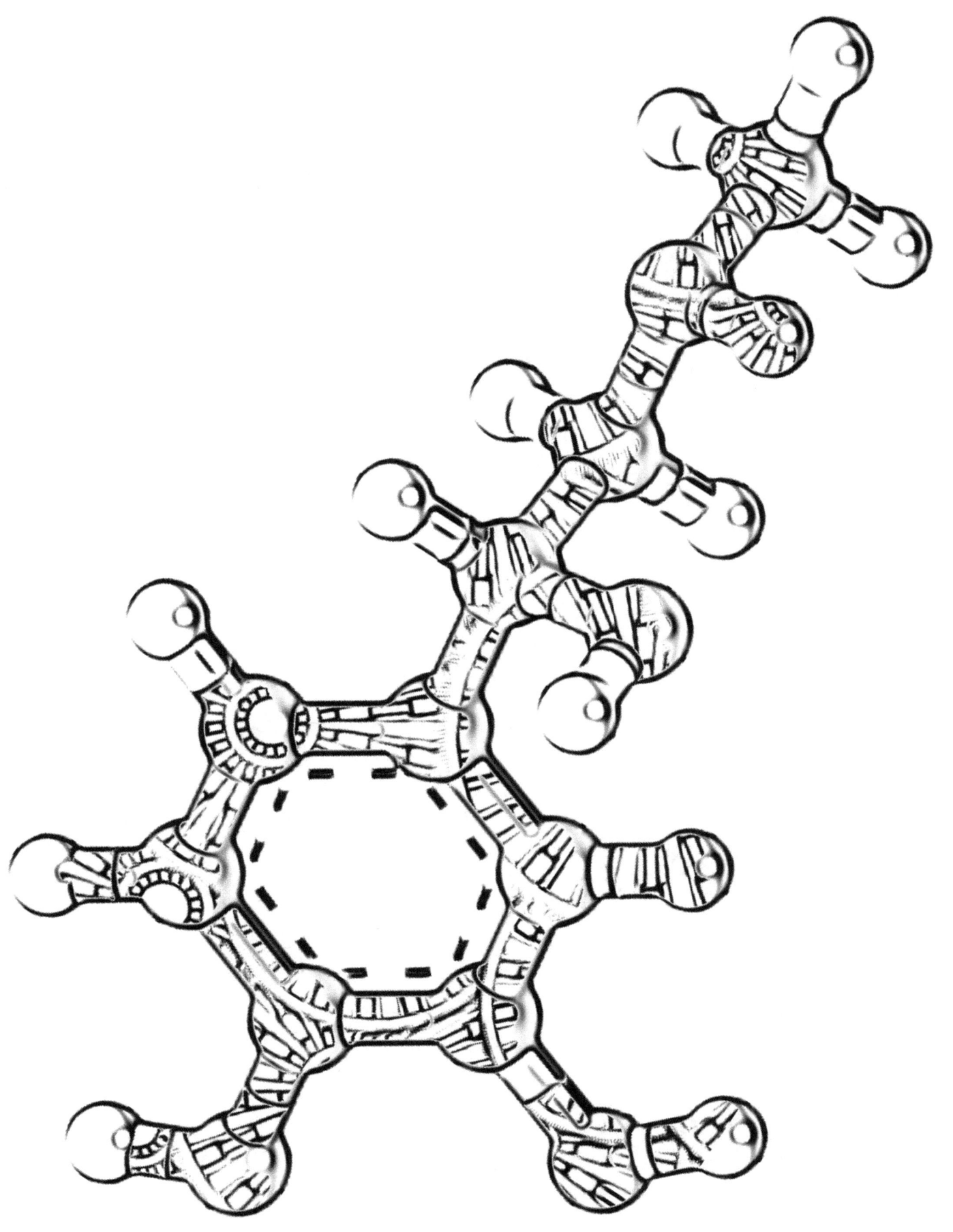

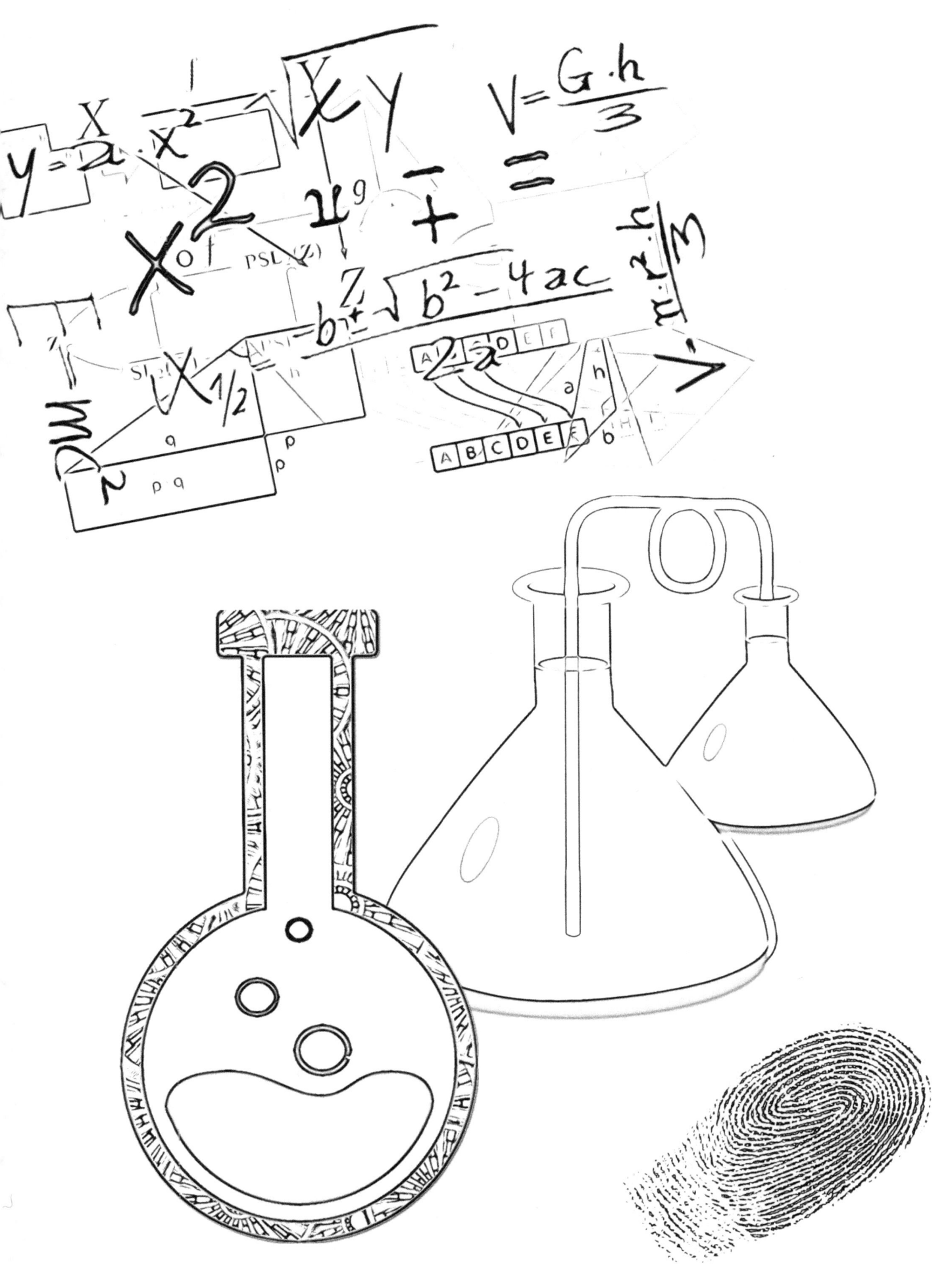

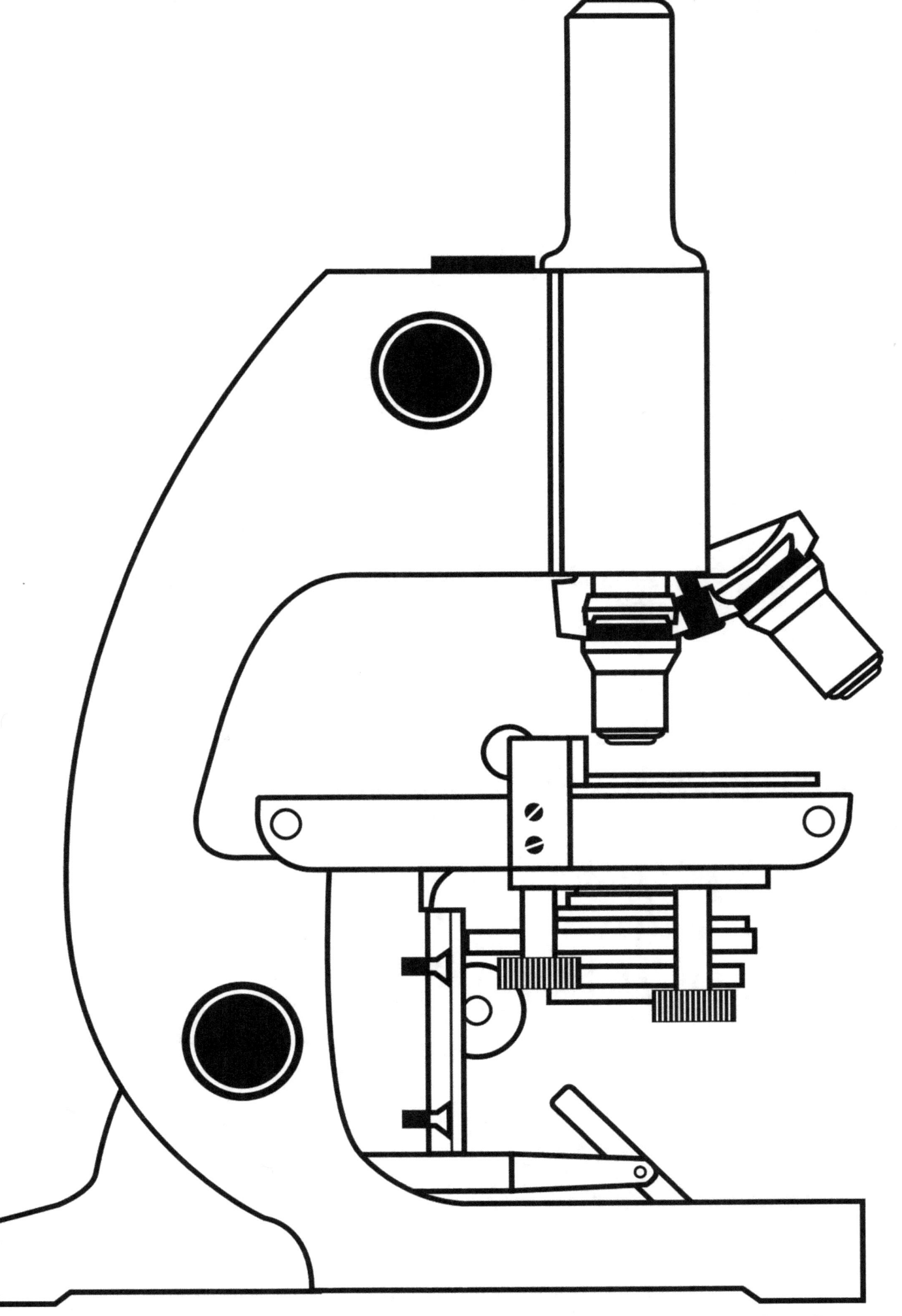

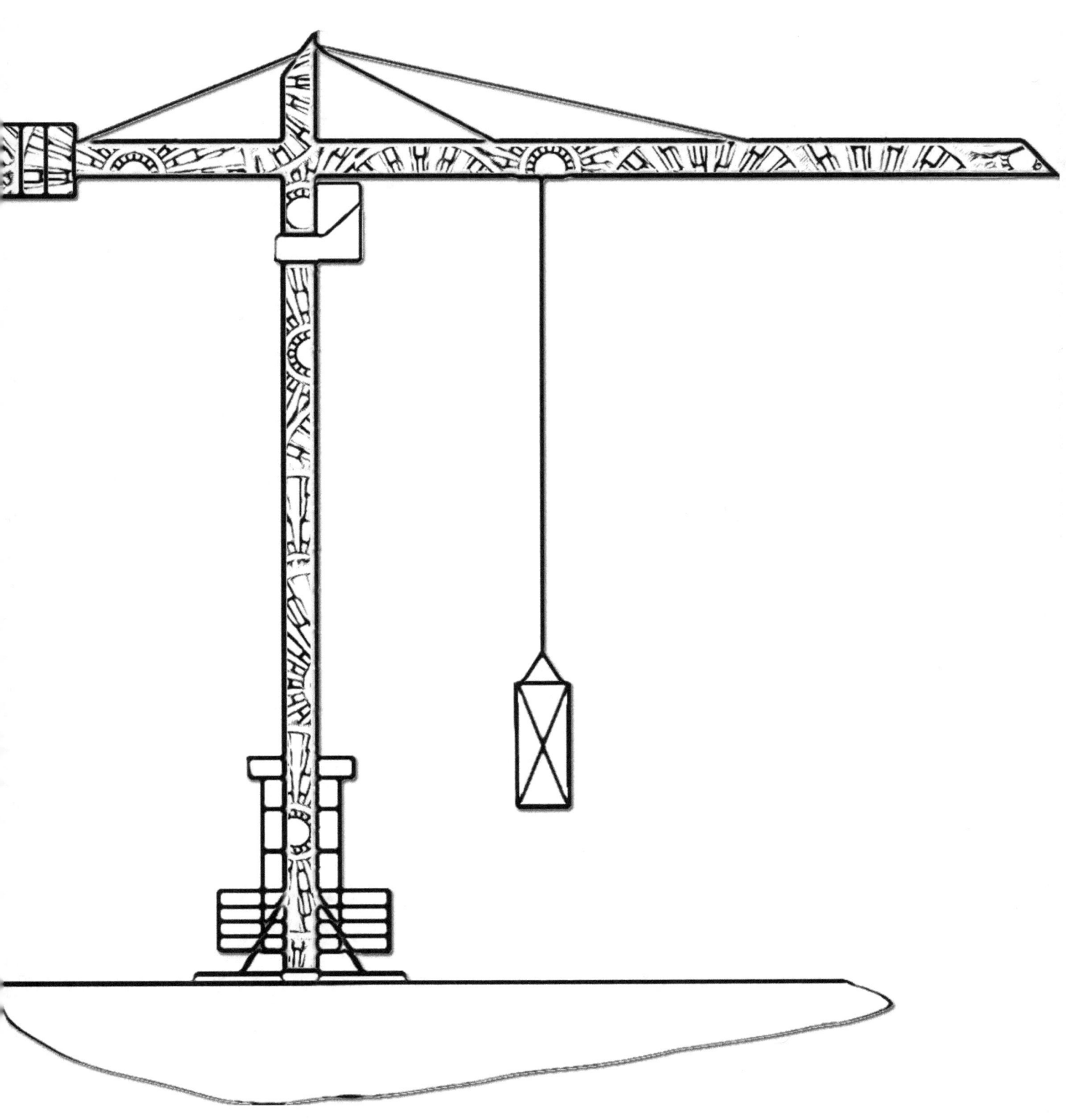

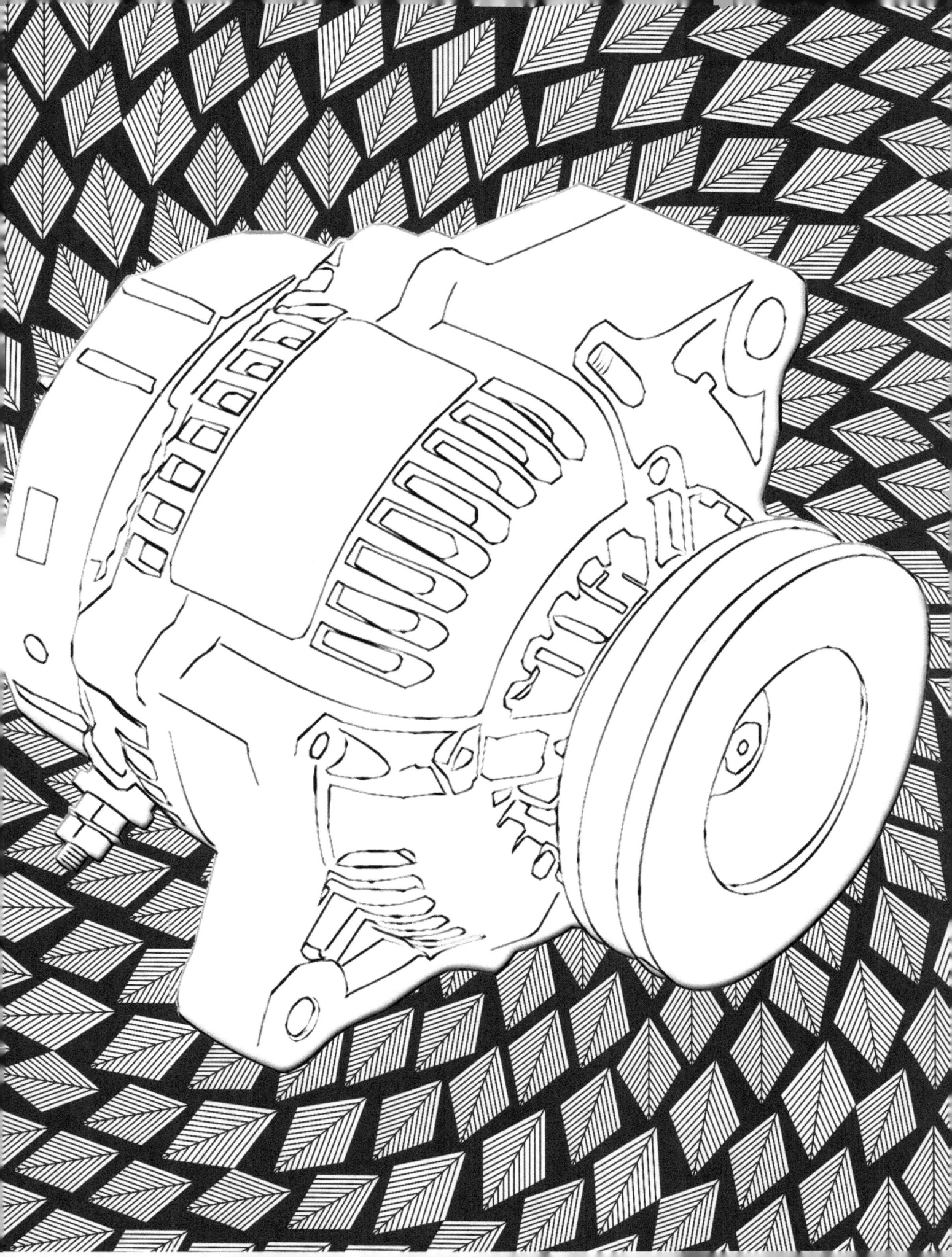

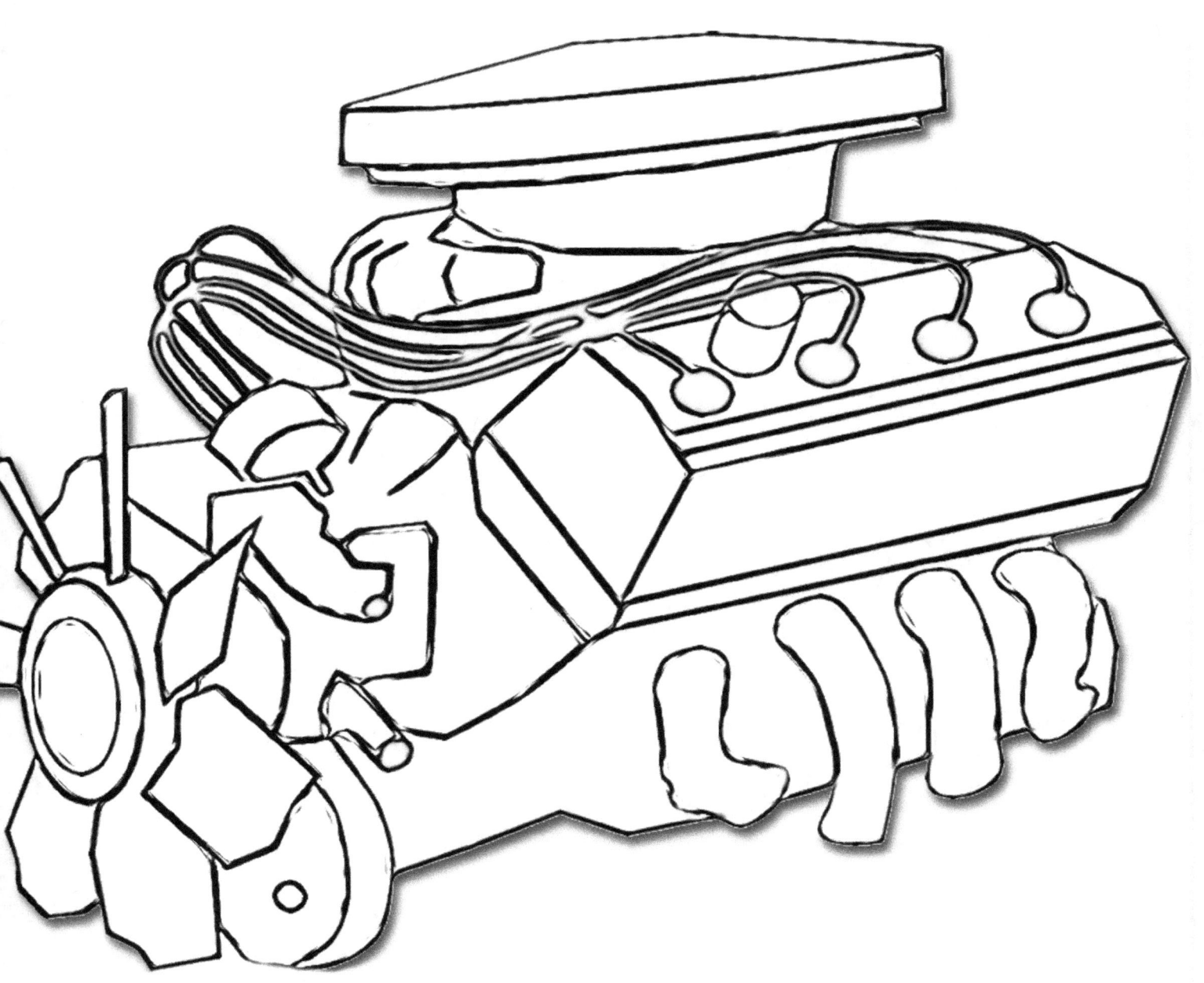

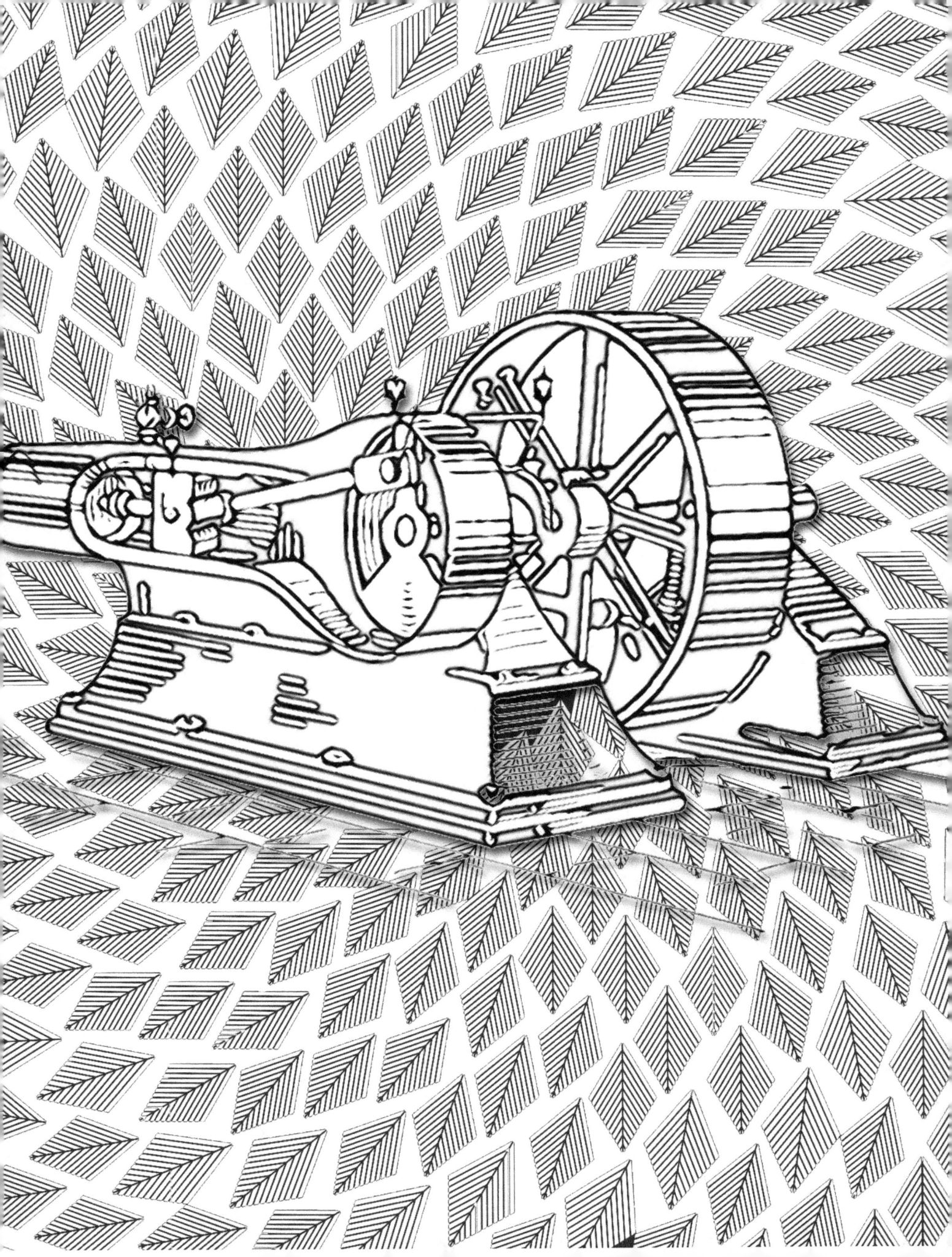

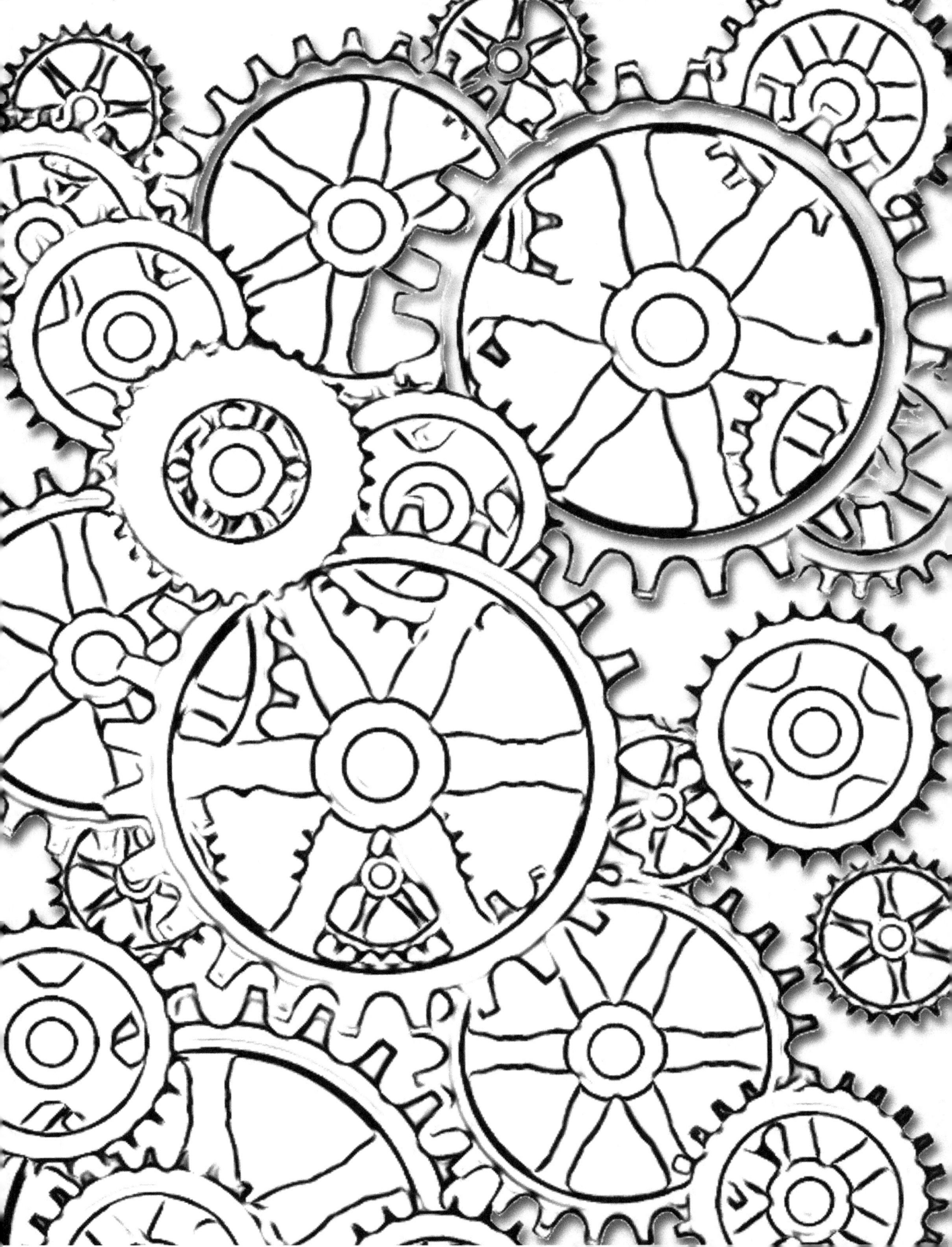

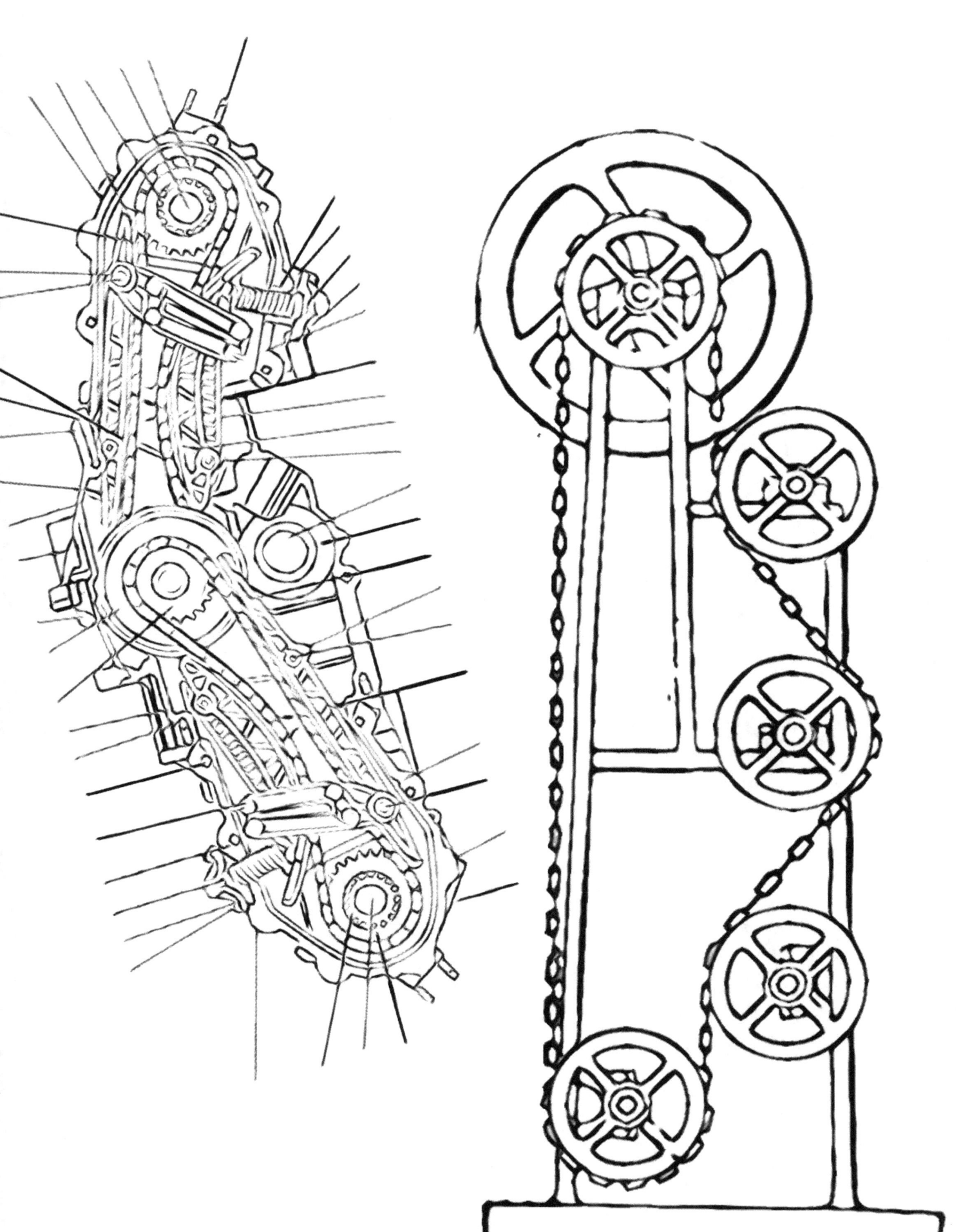

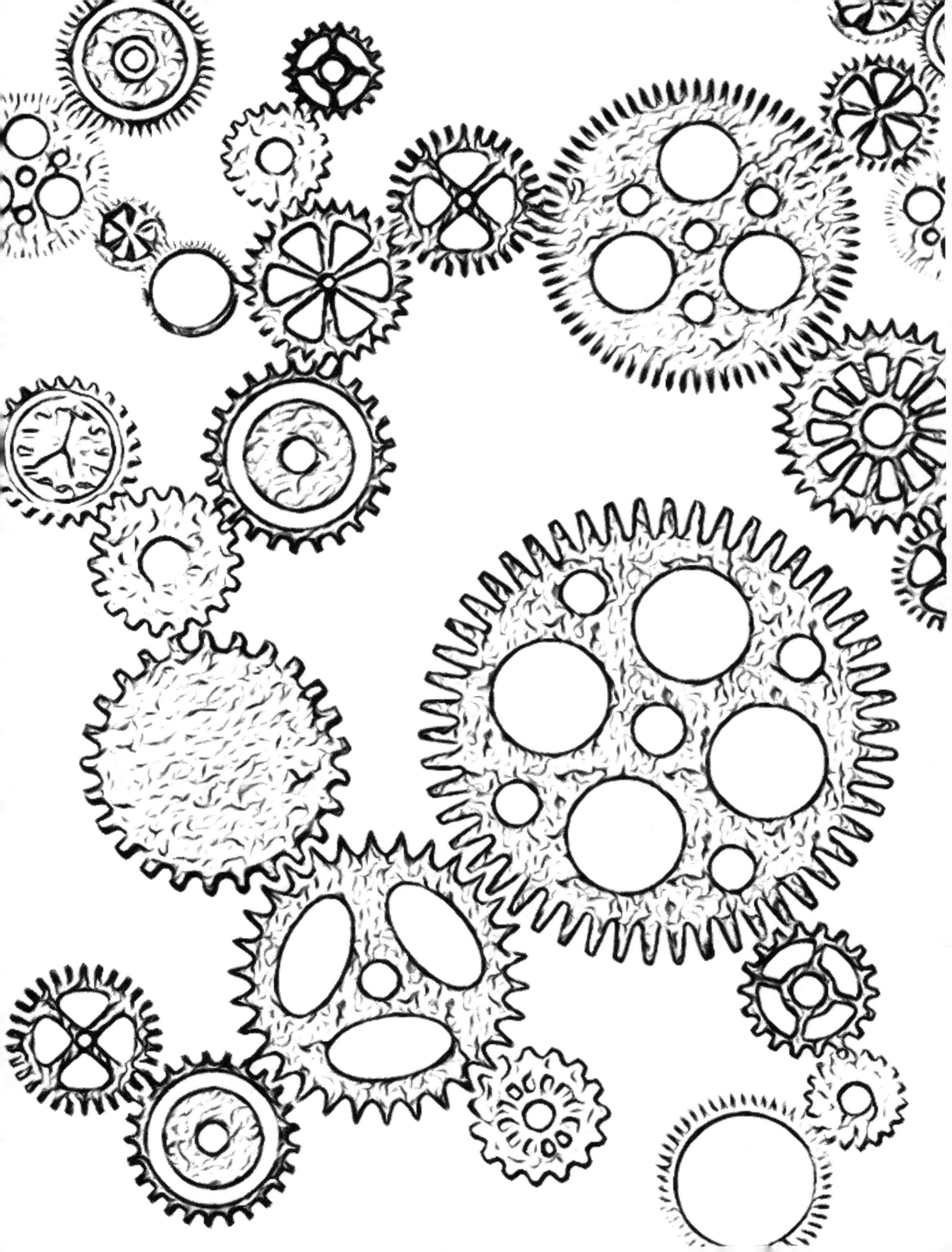

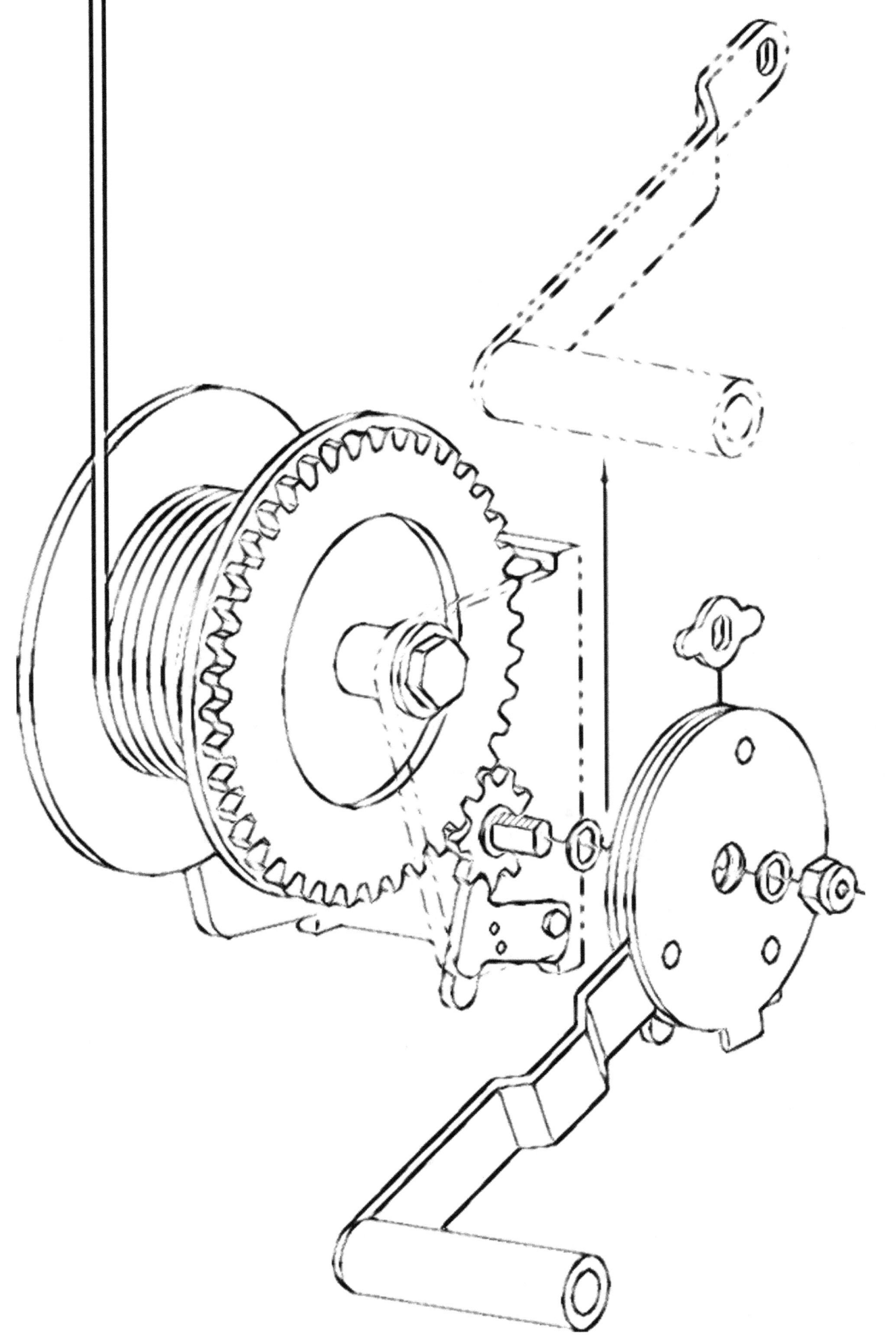

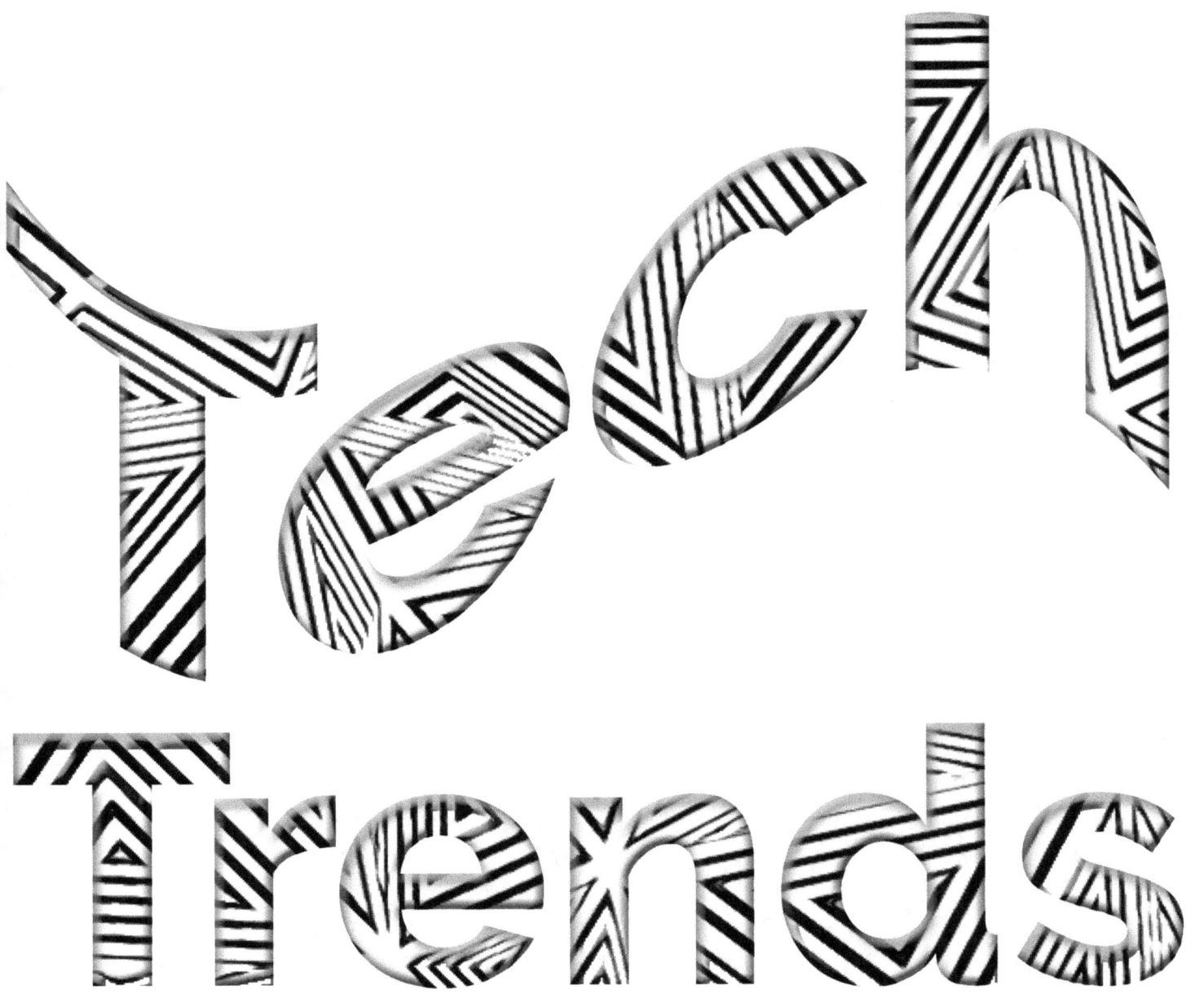

Then and now

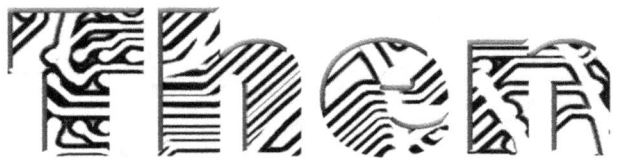
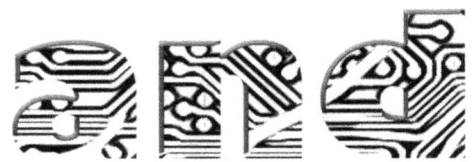
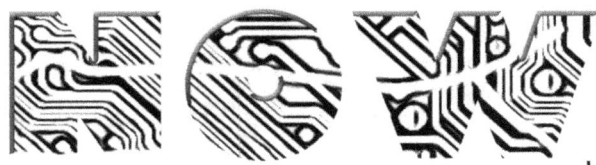

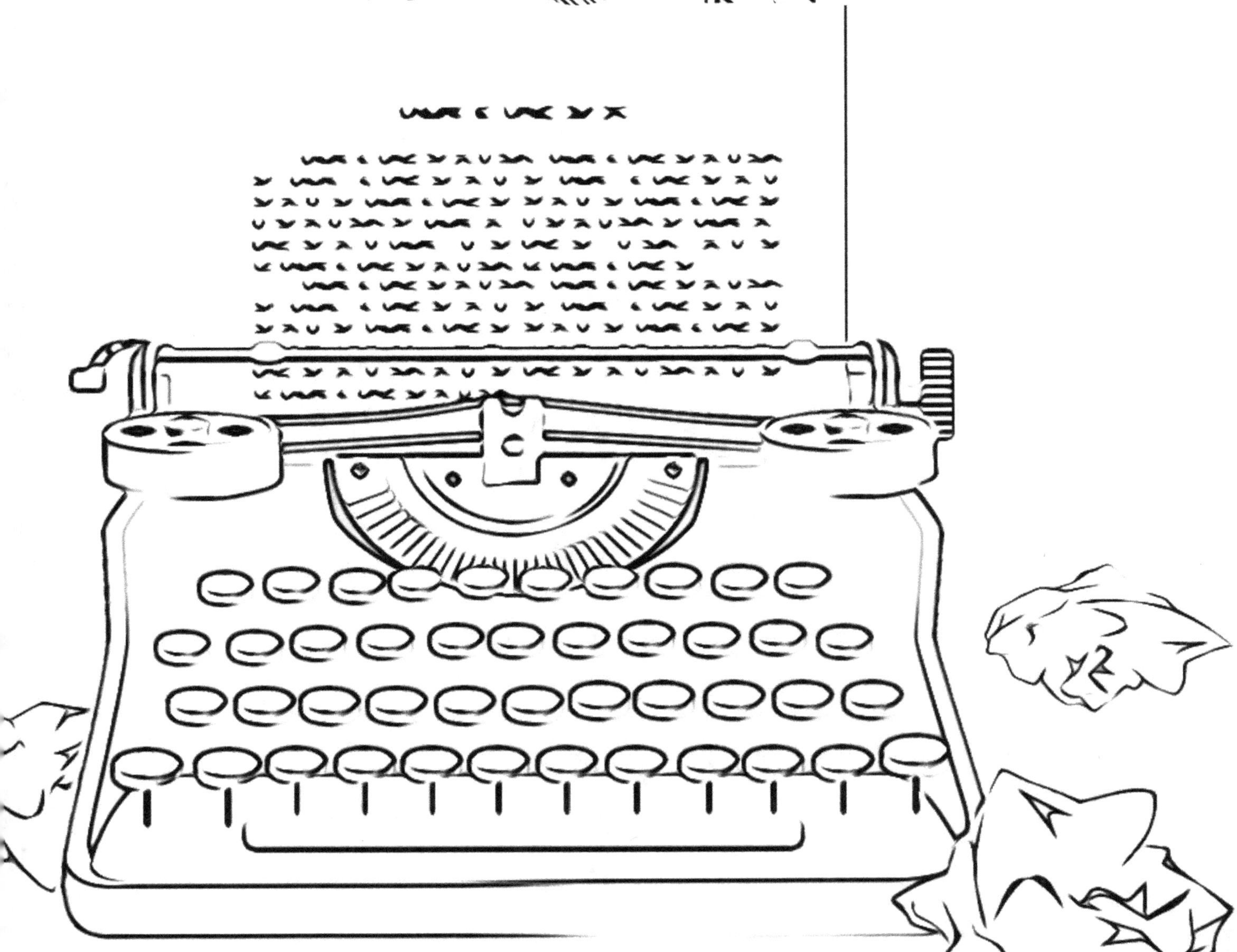

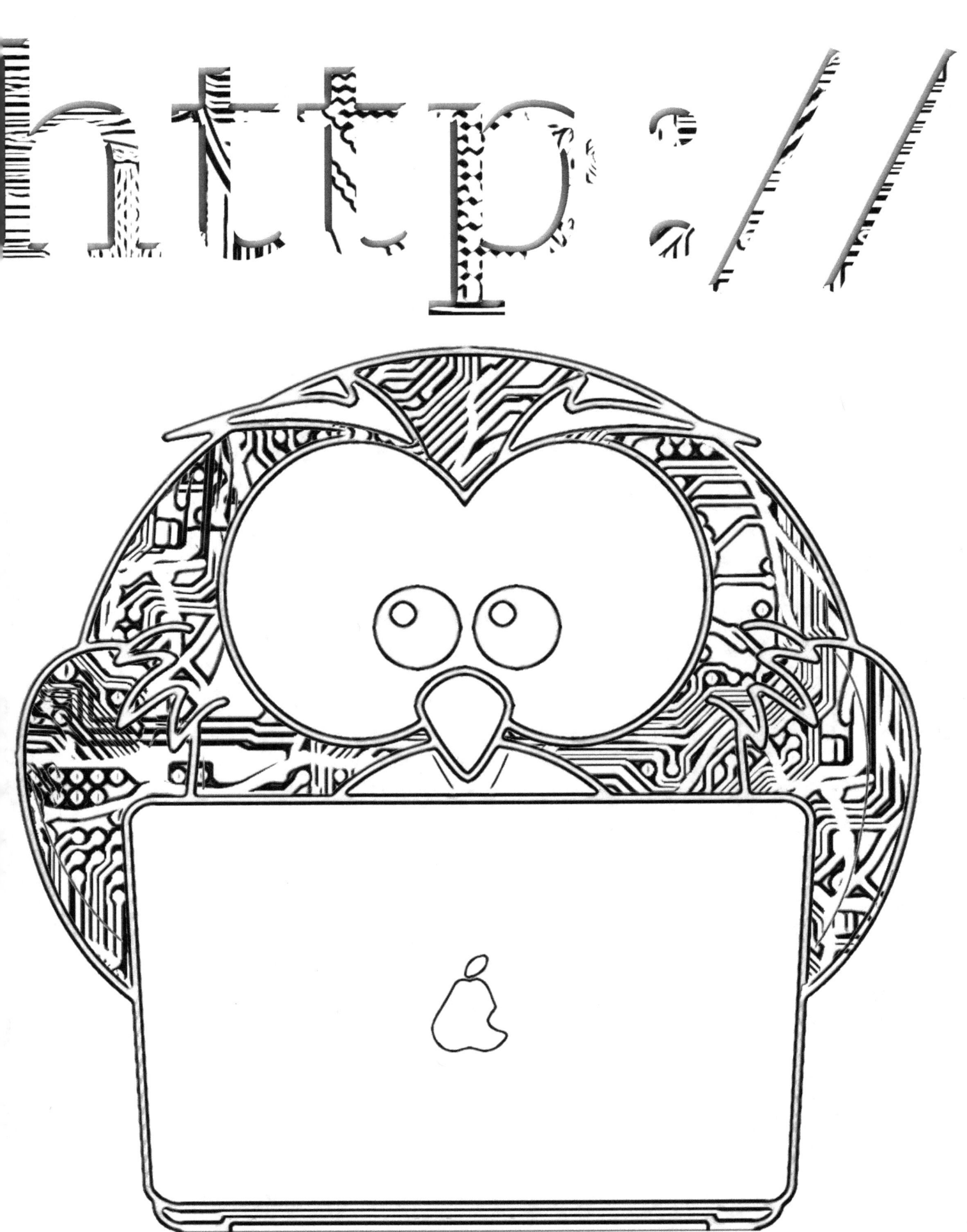

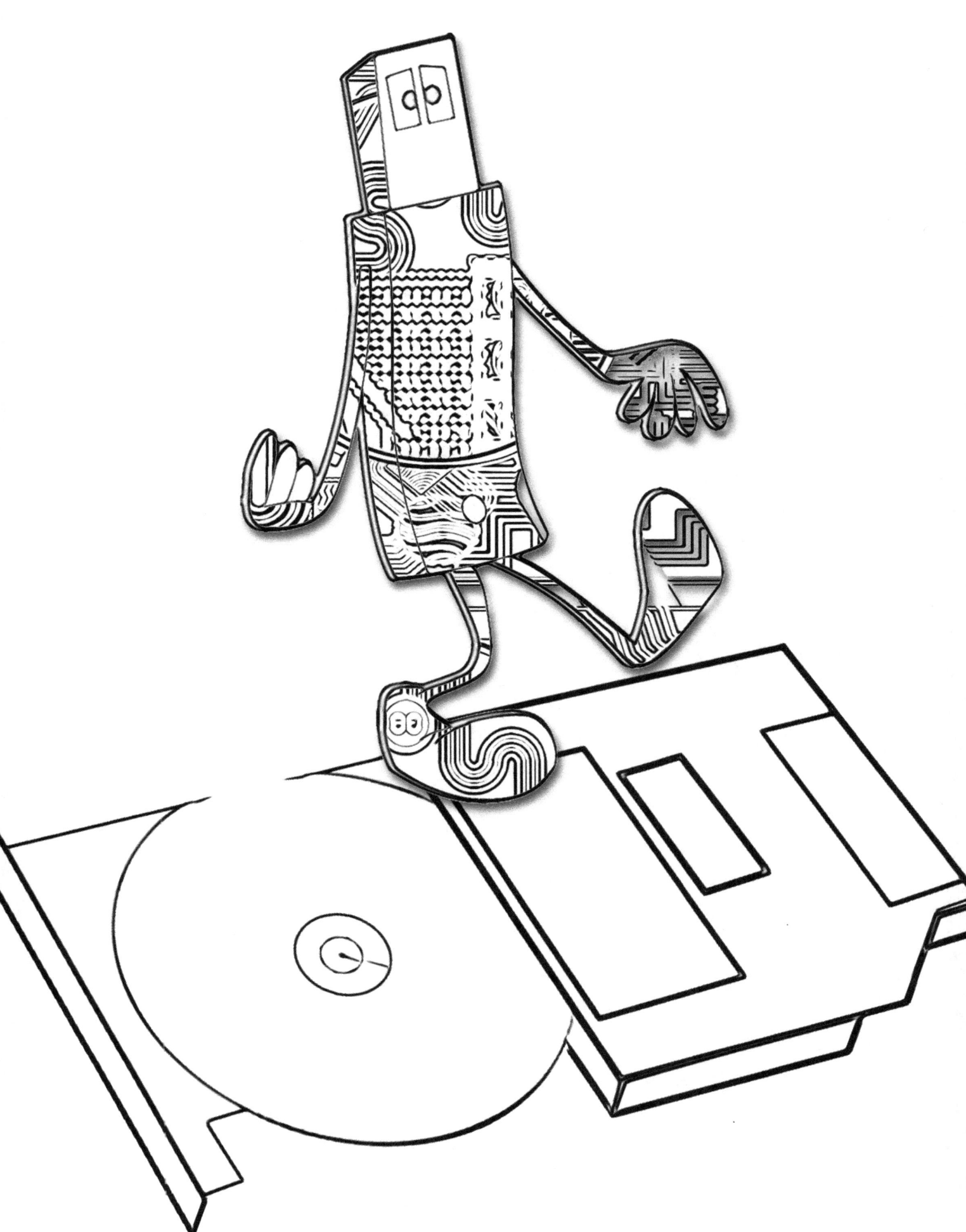

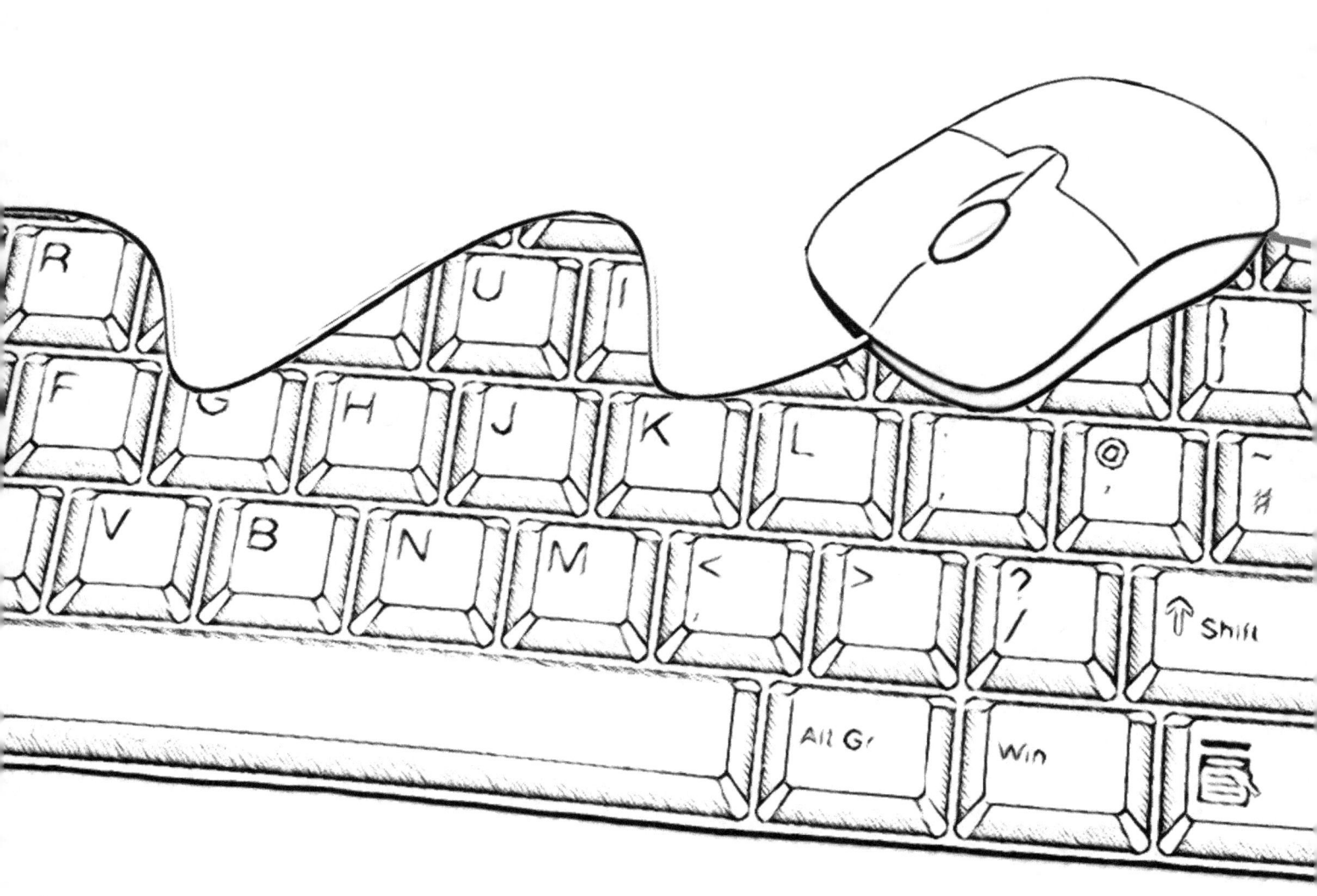

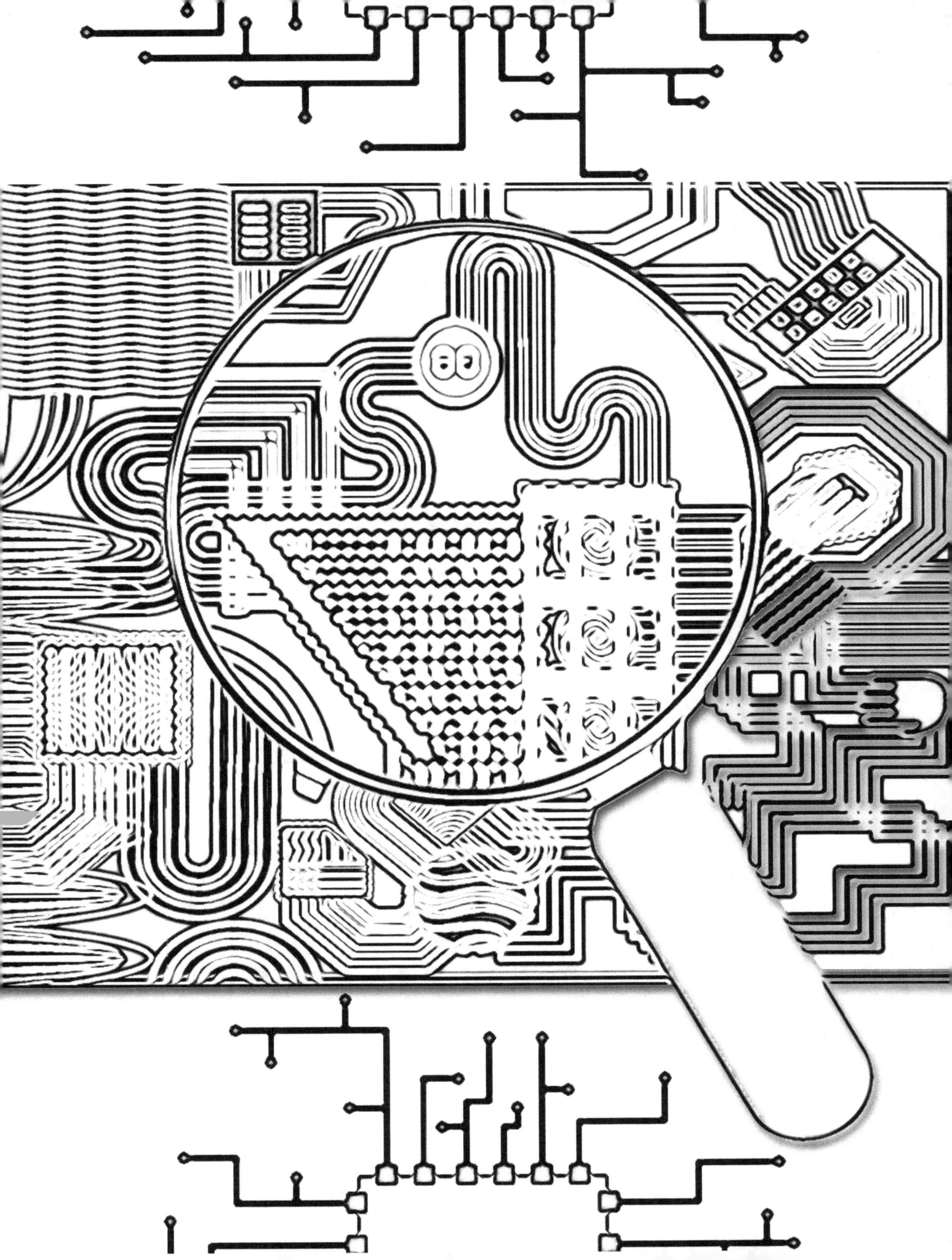

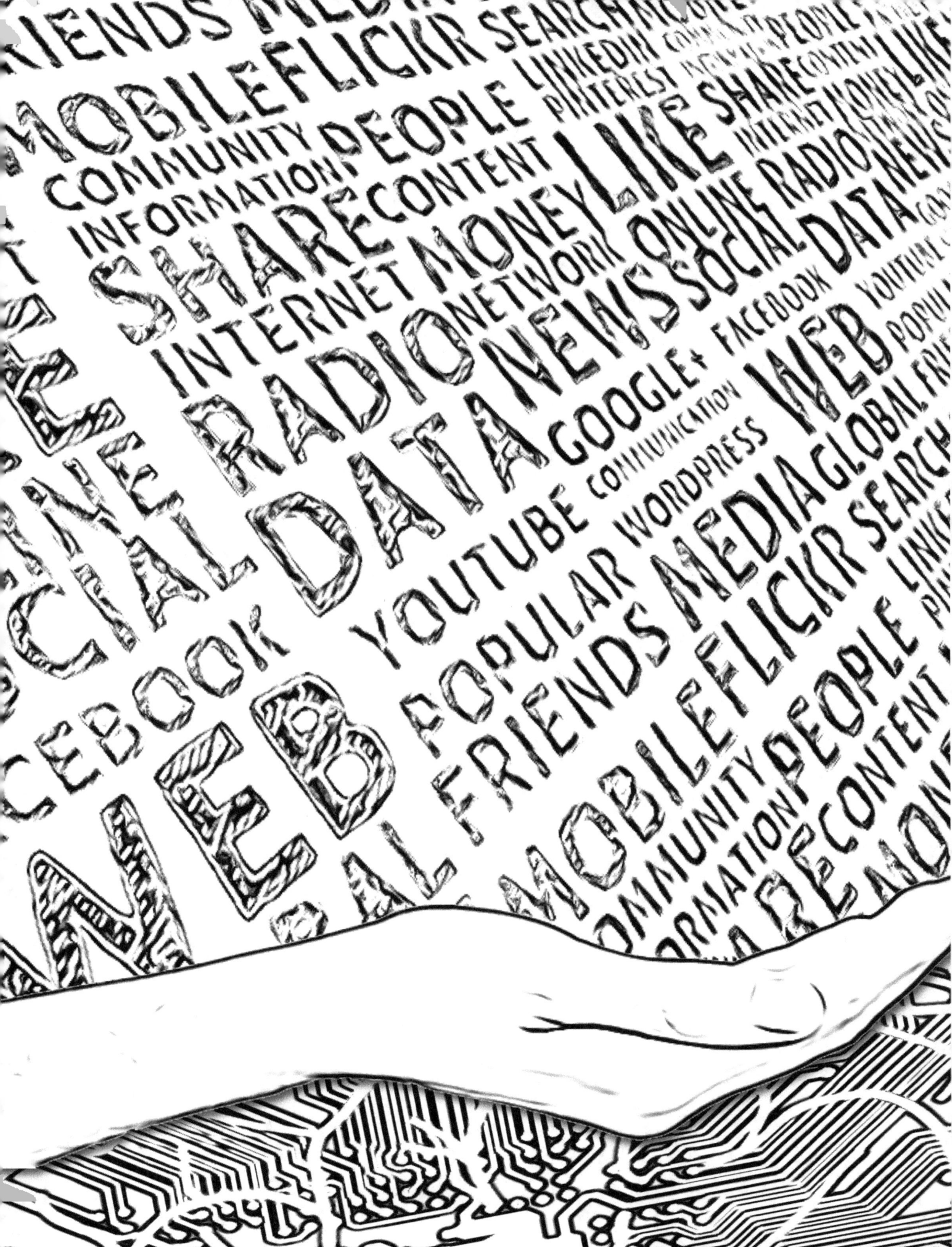

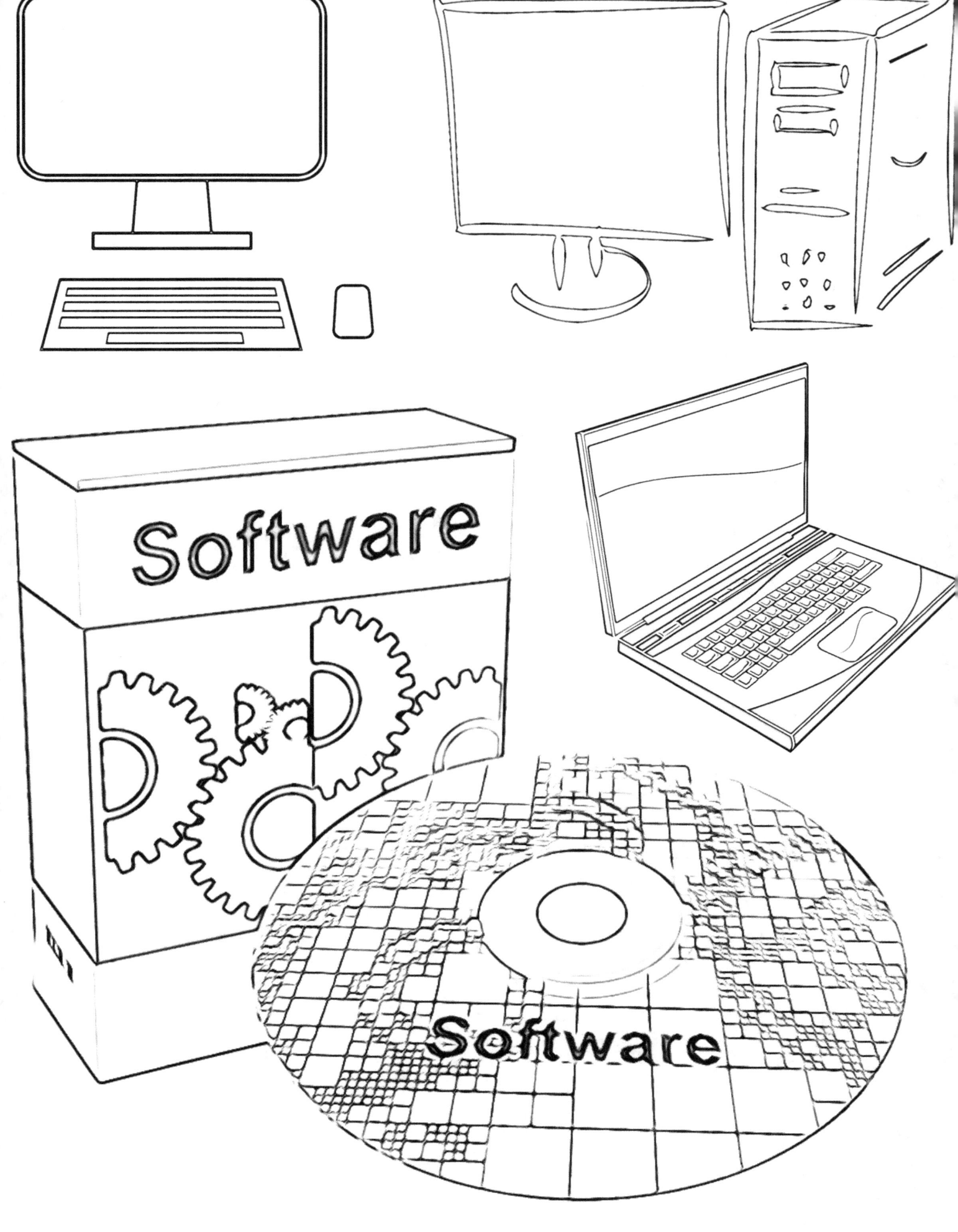

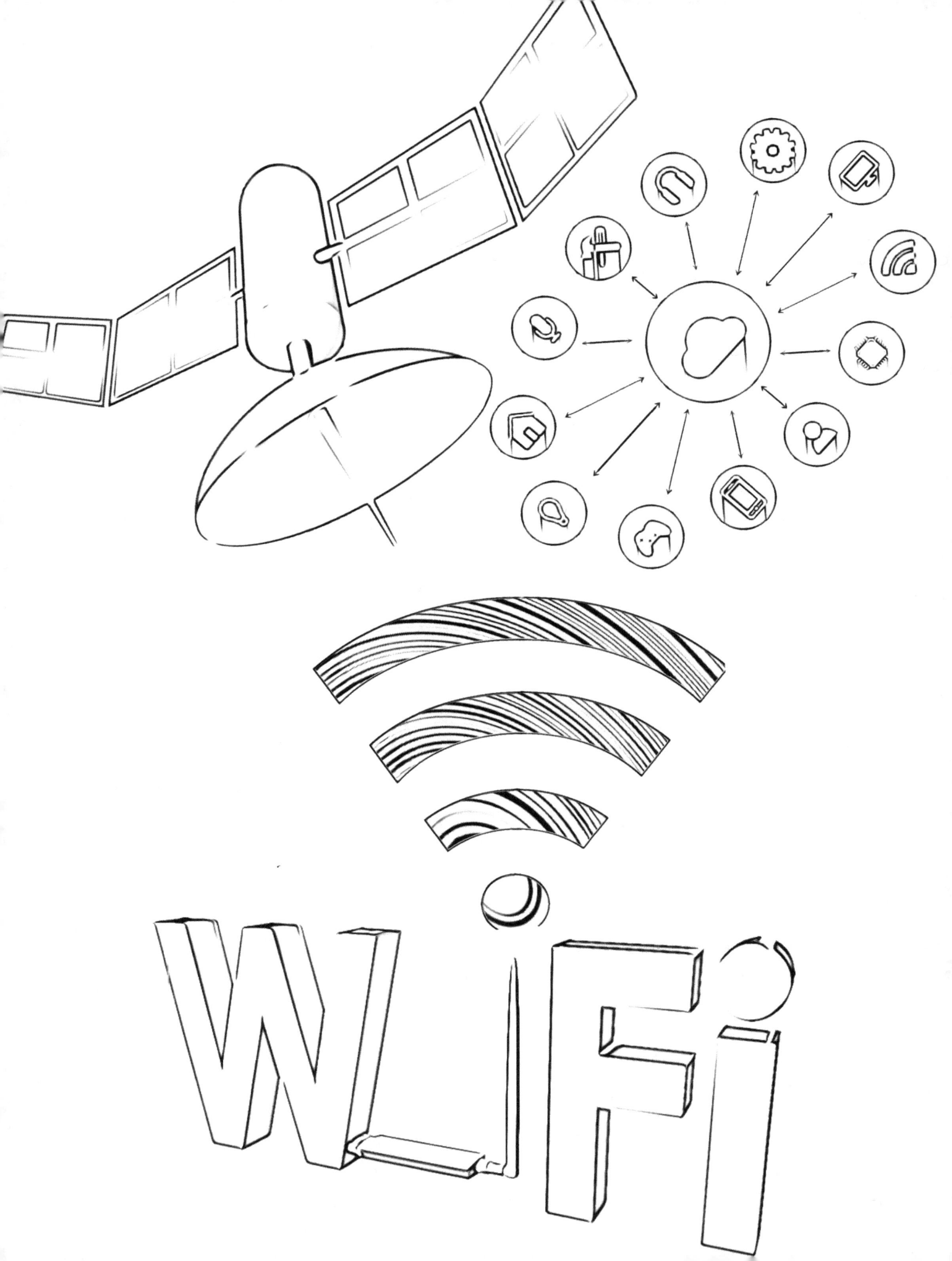

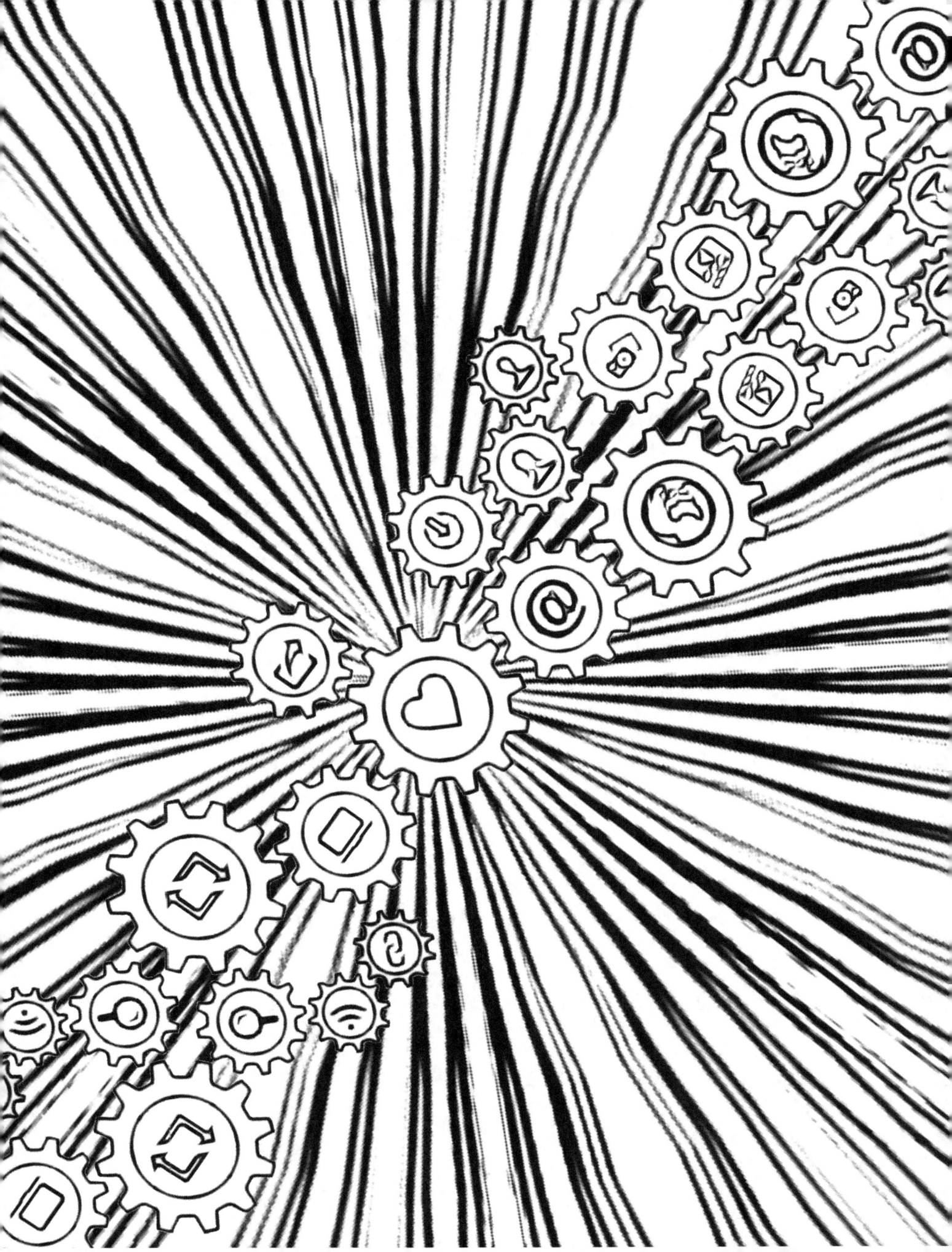

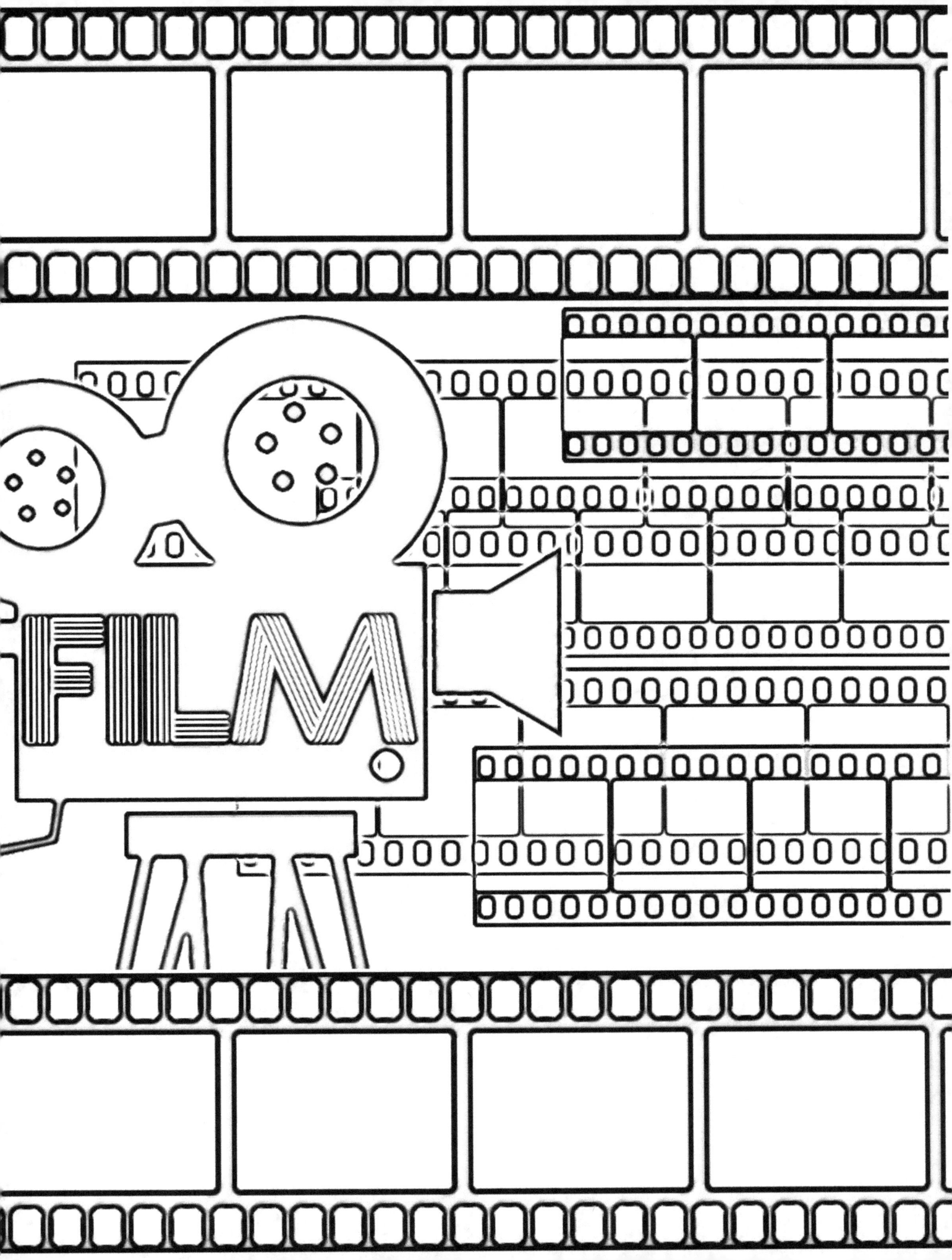

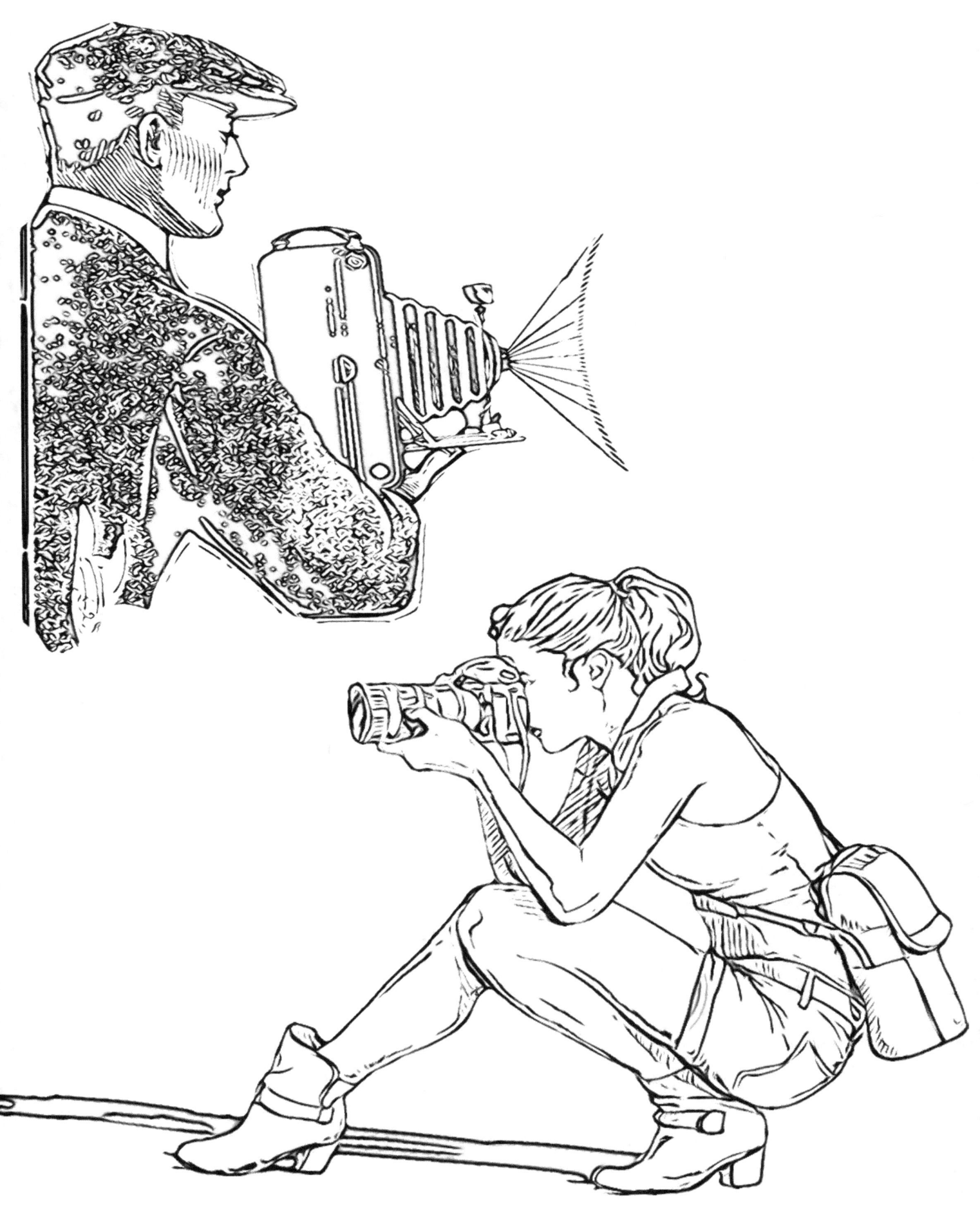

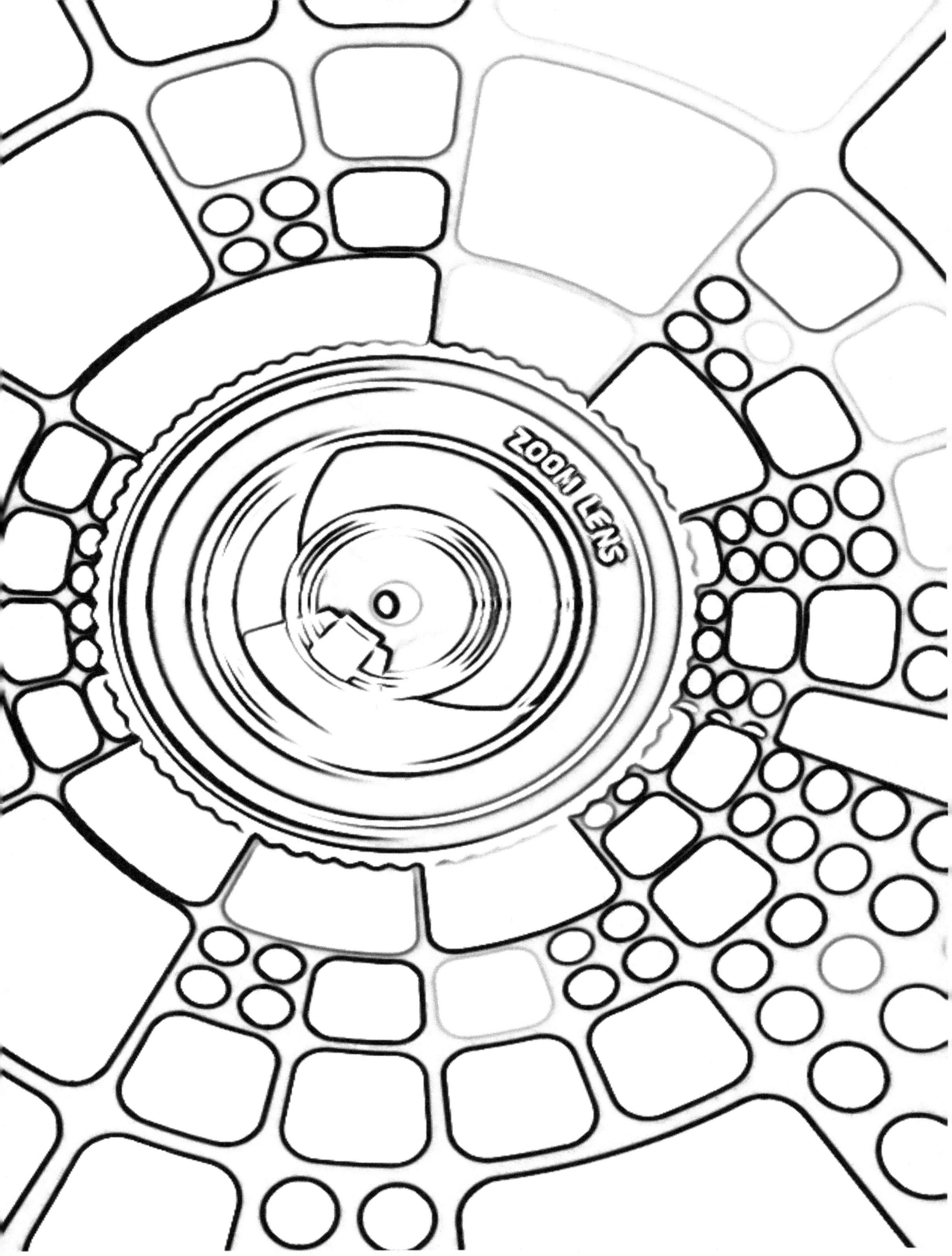

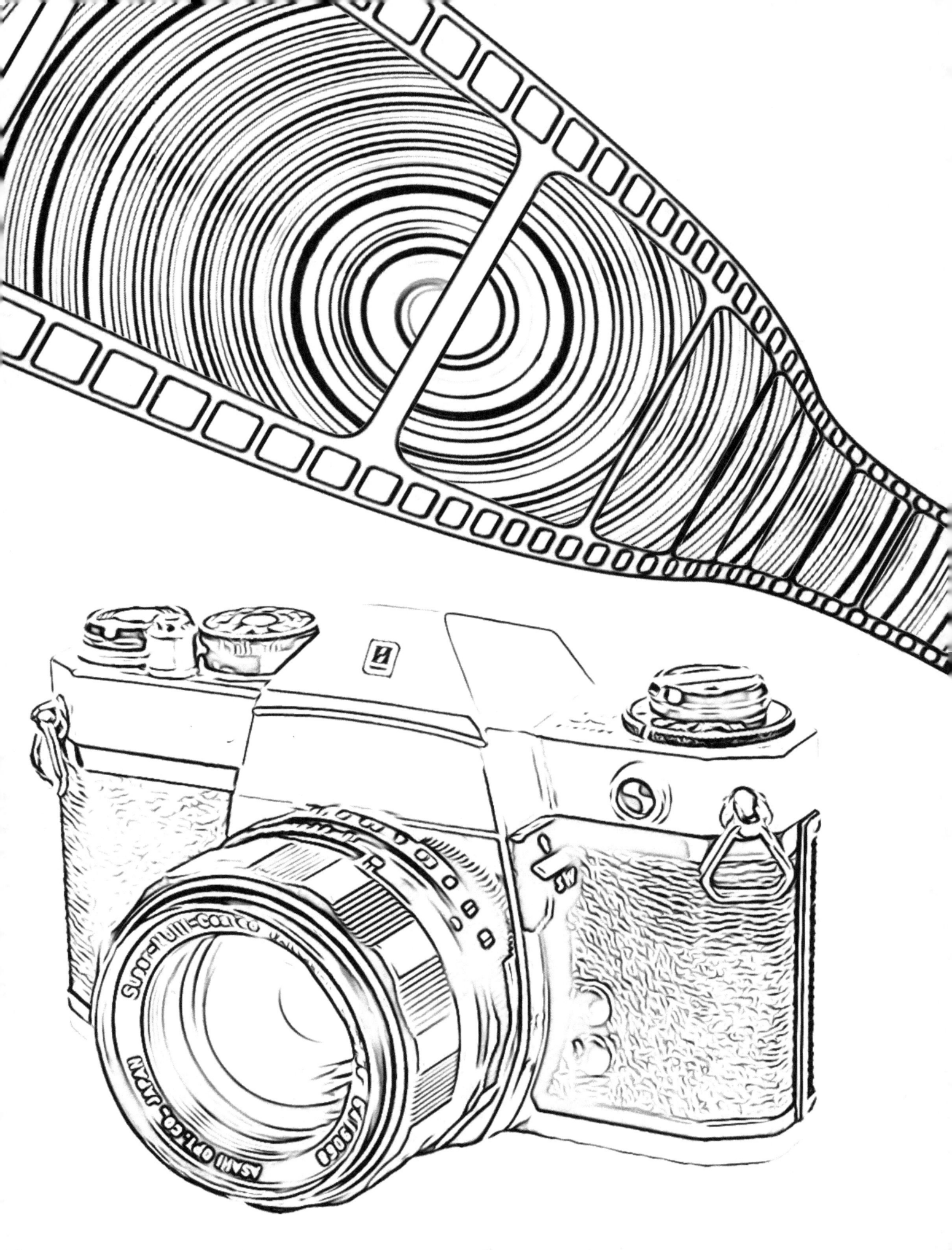

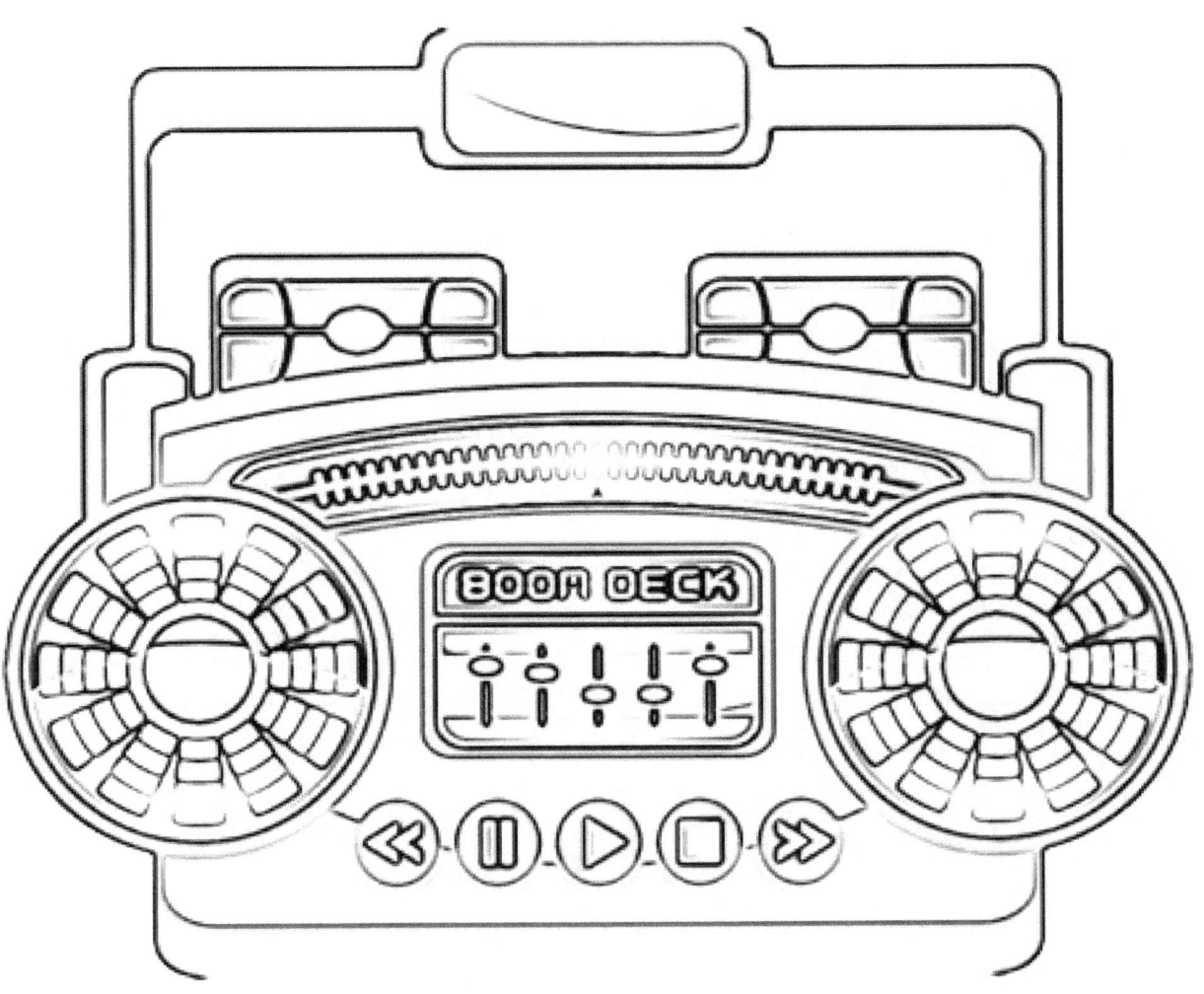

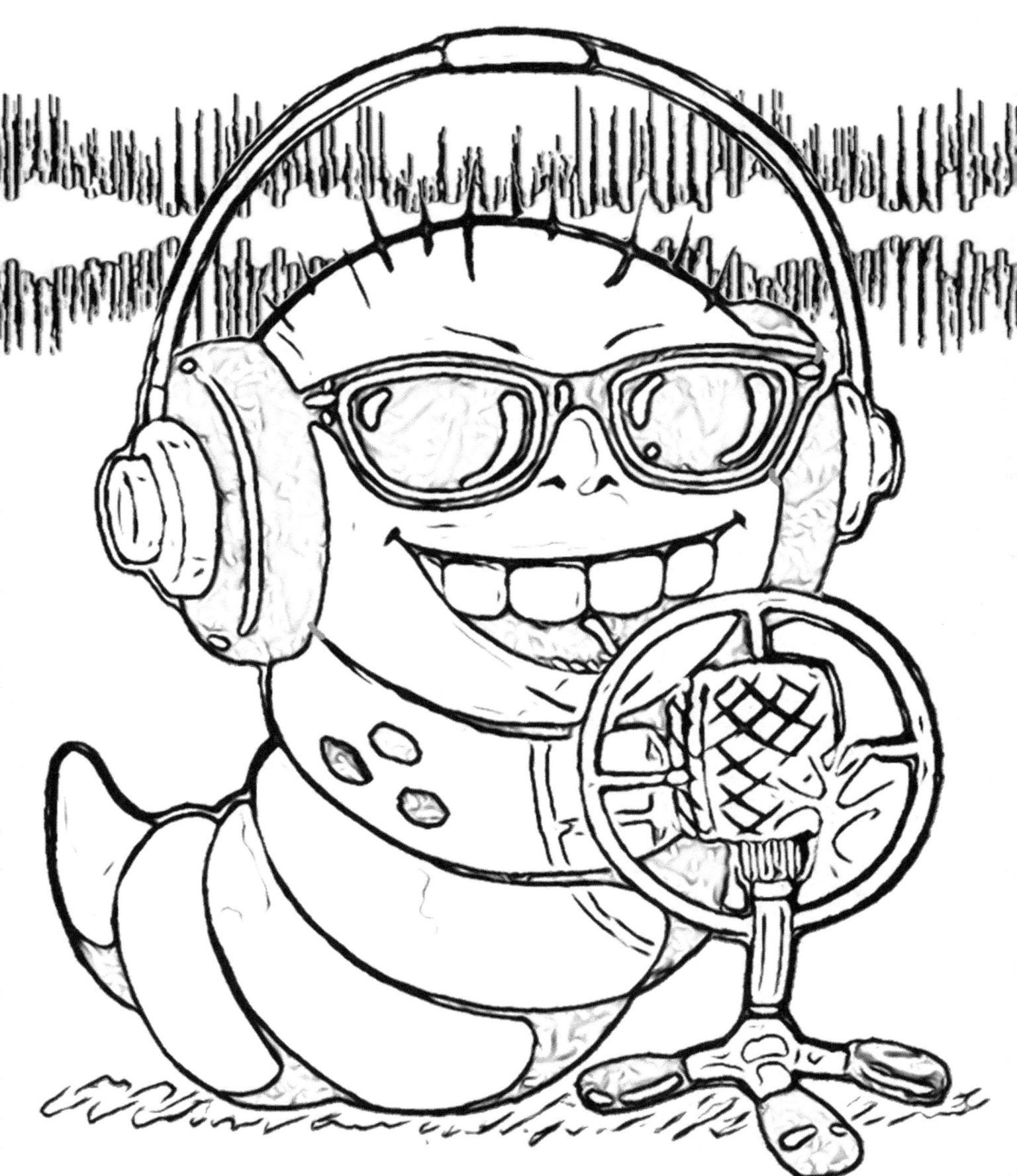

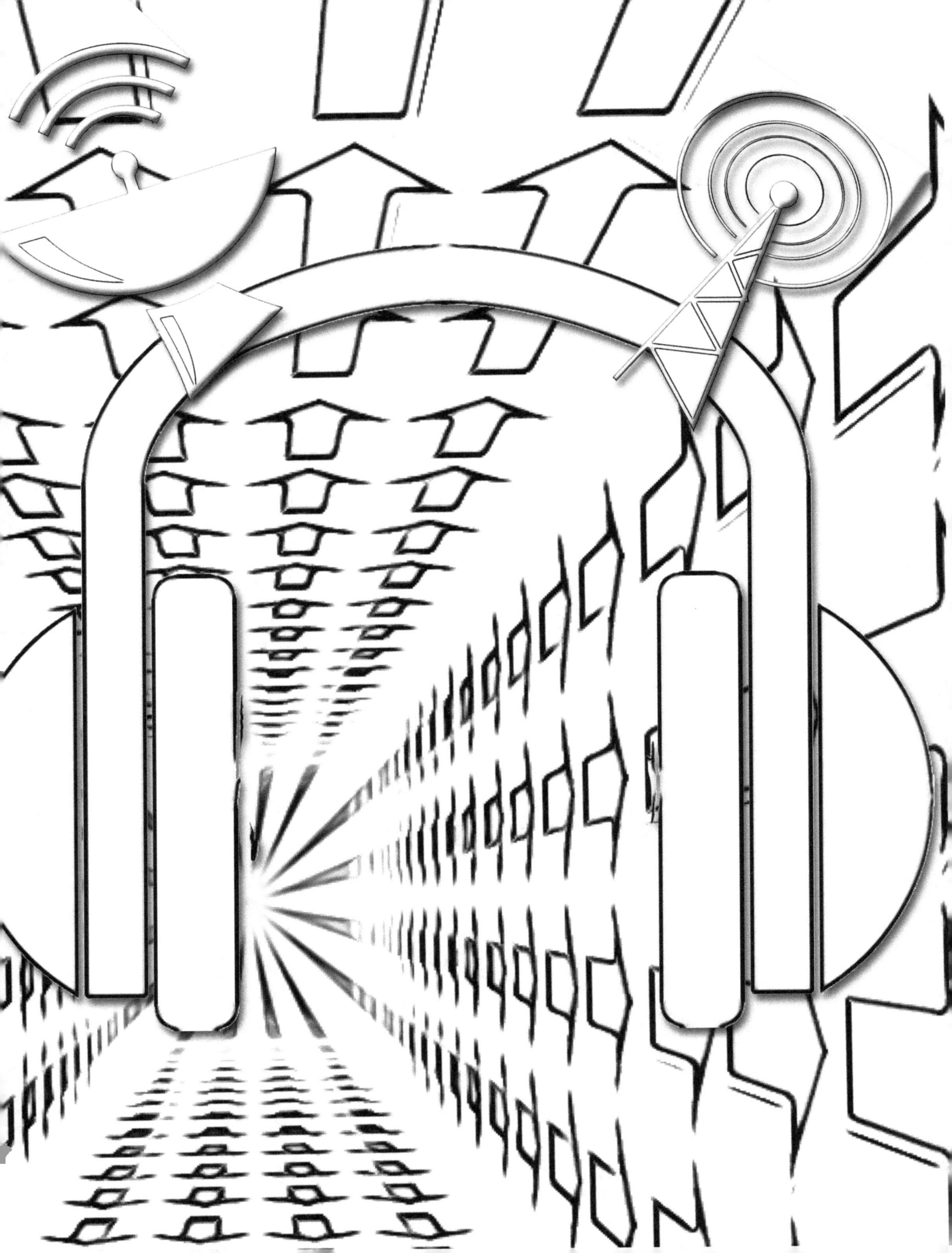

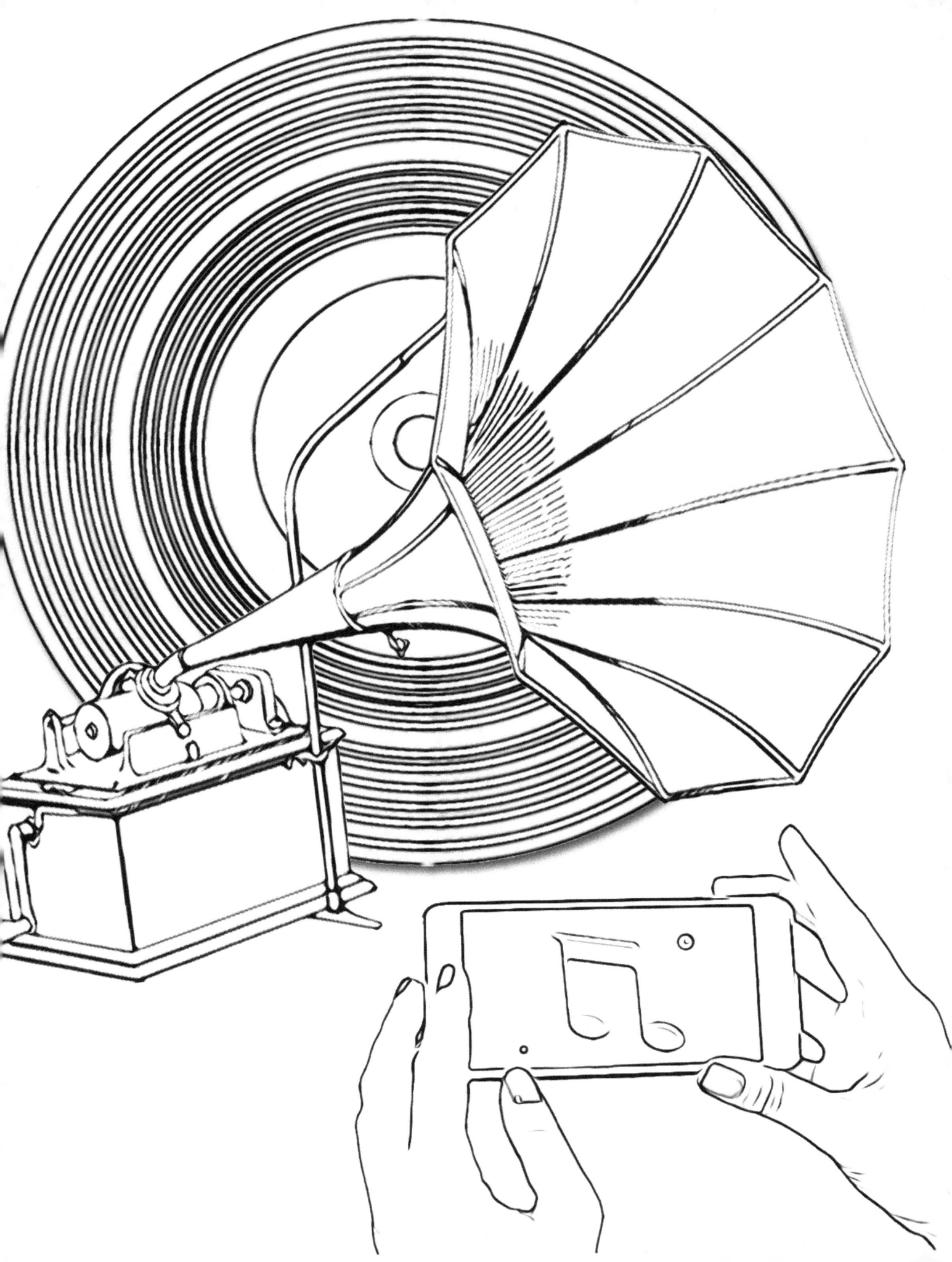

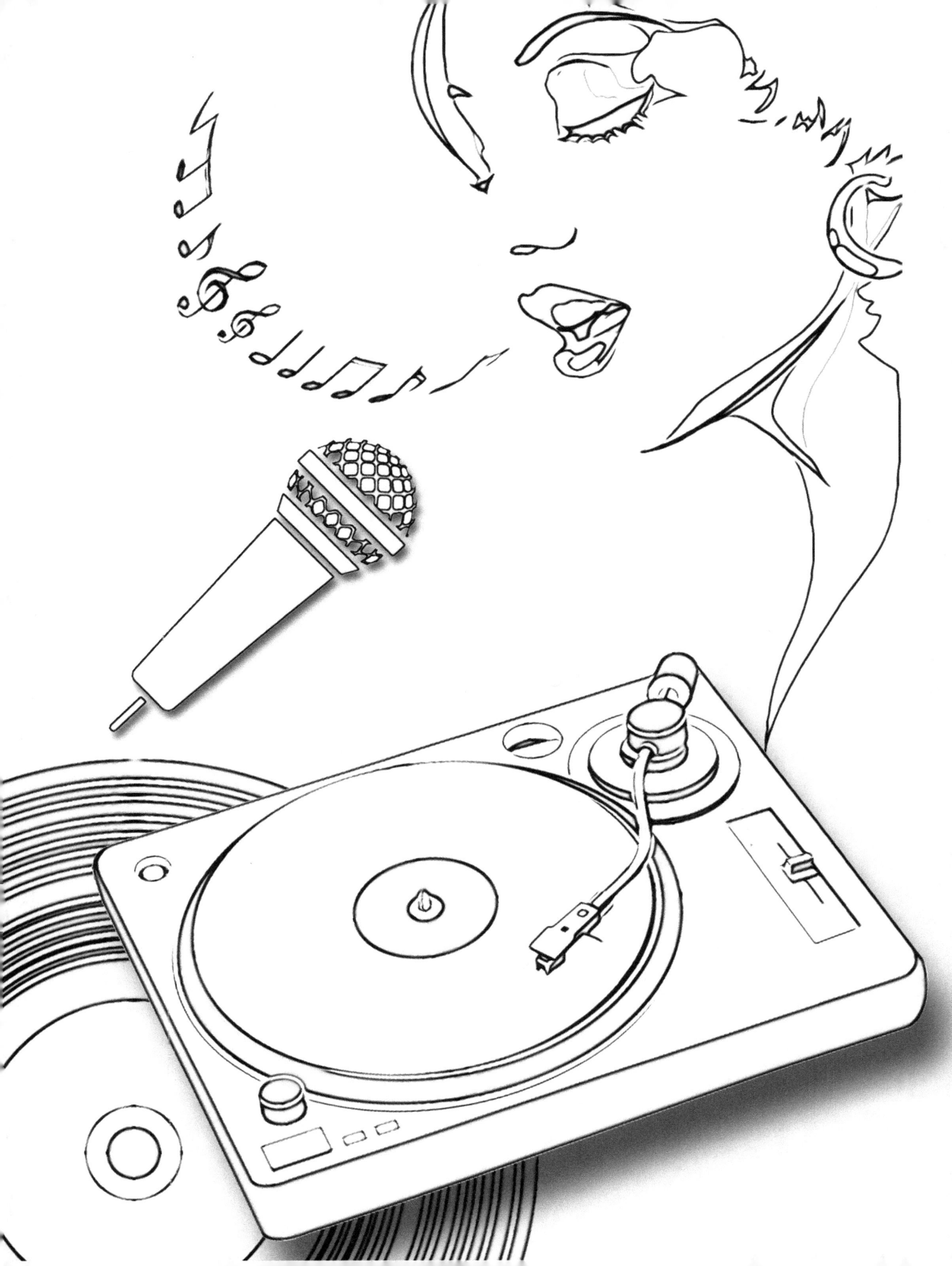

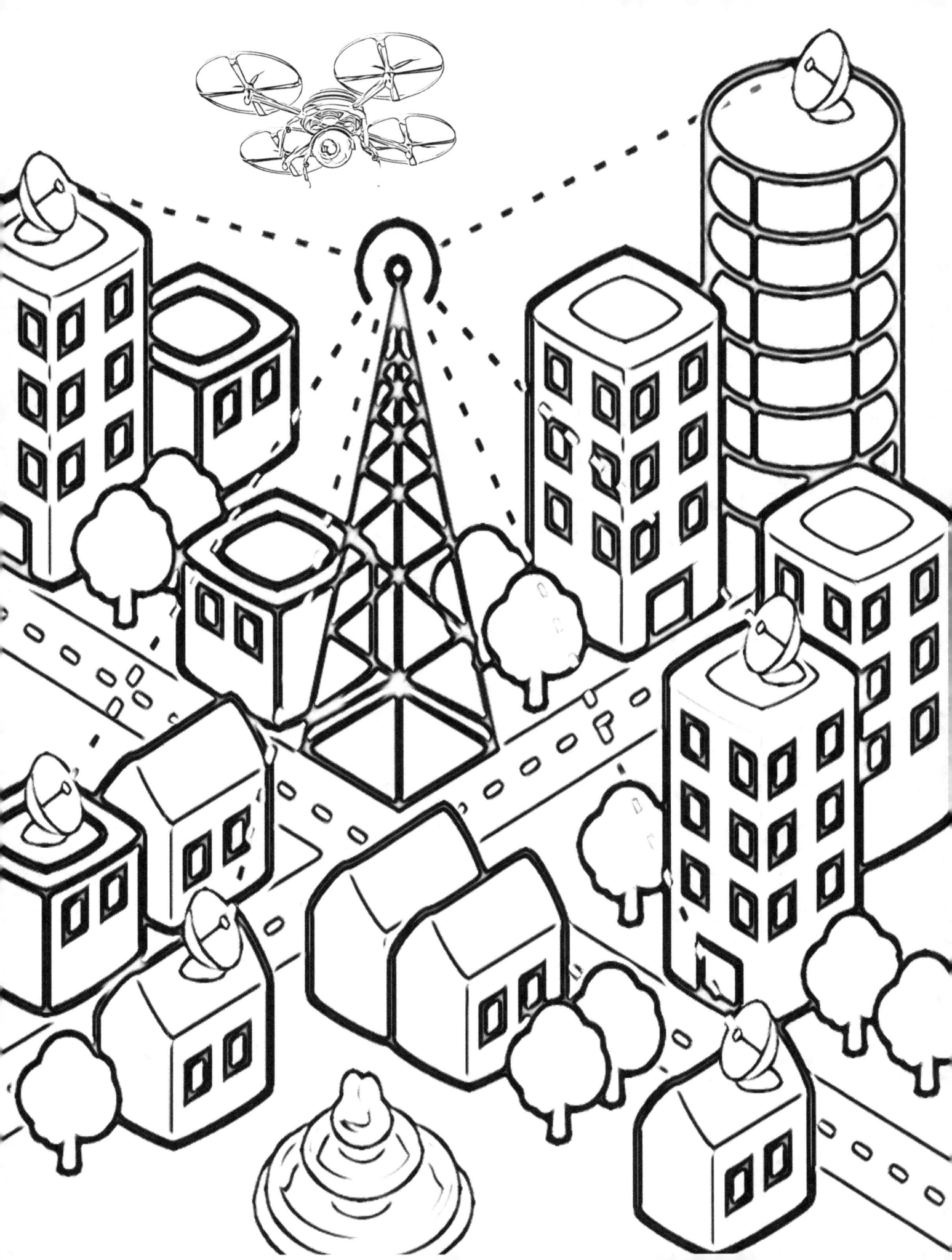

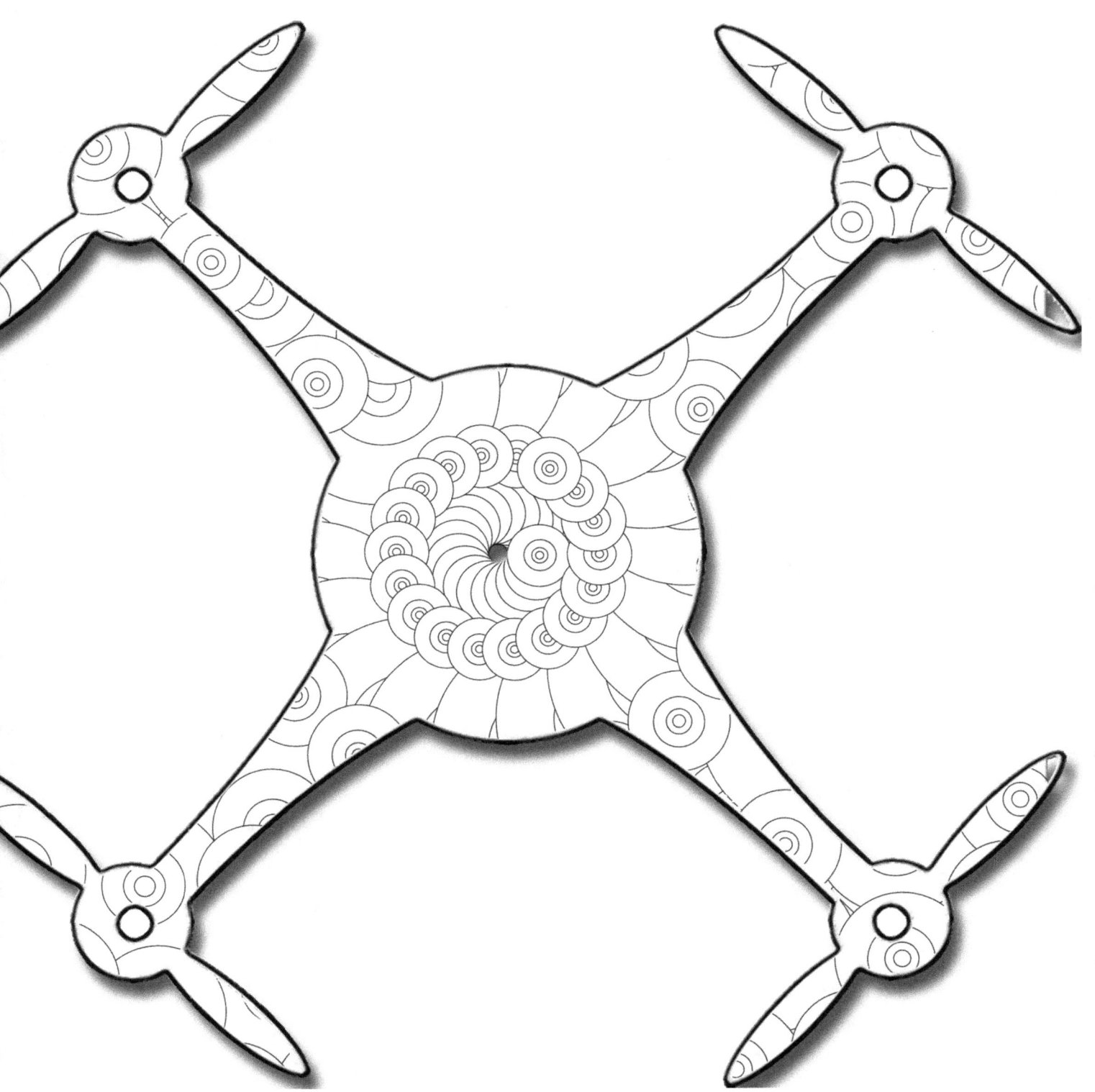

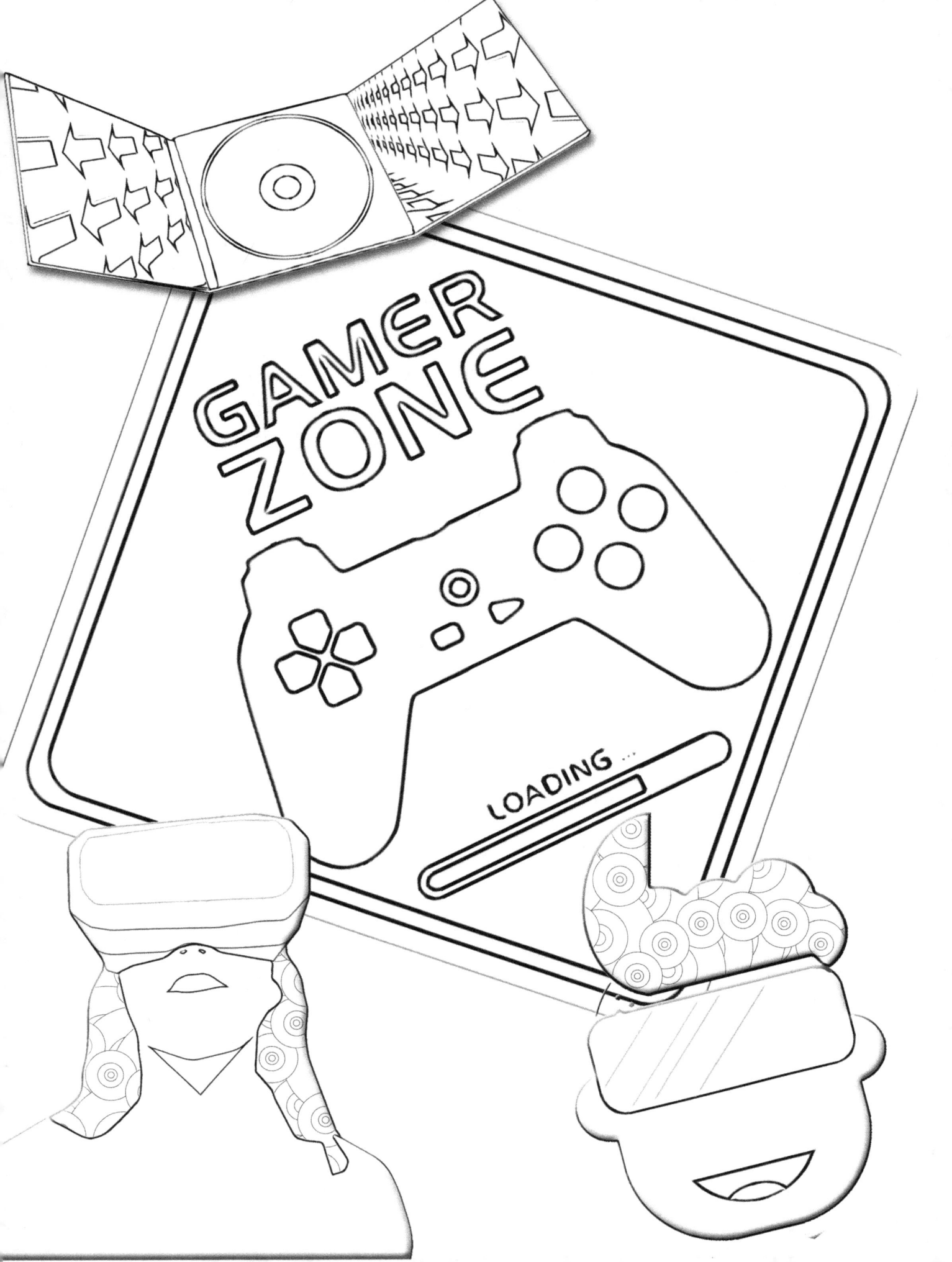

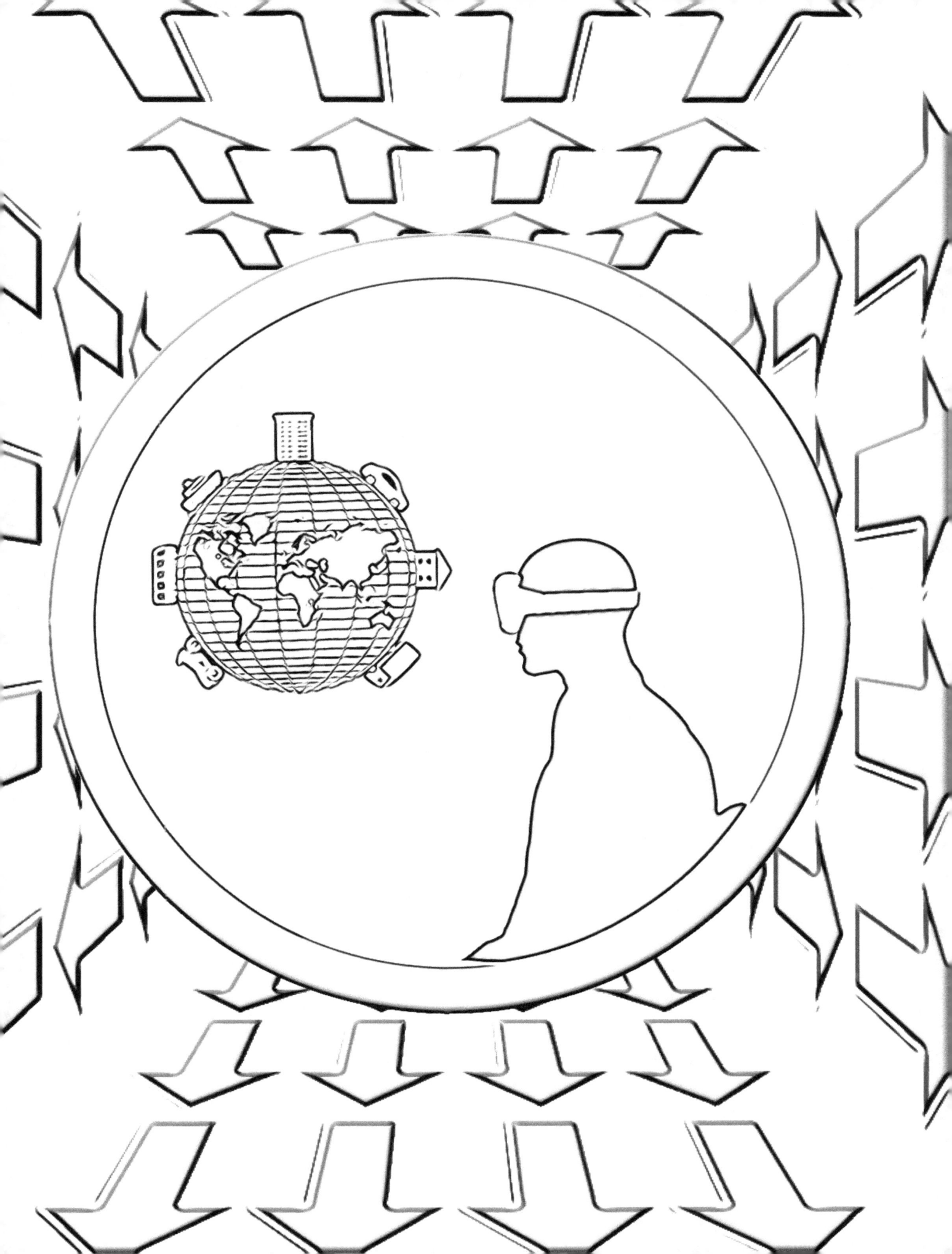

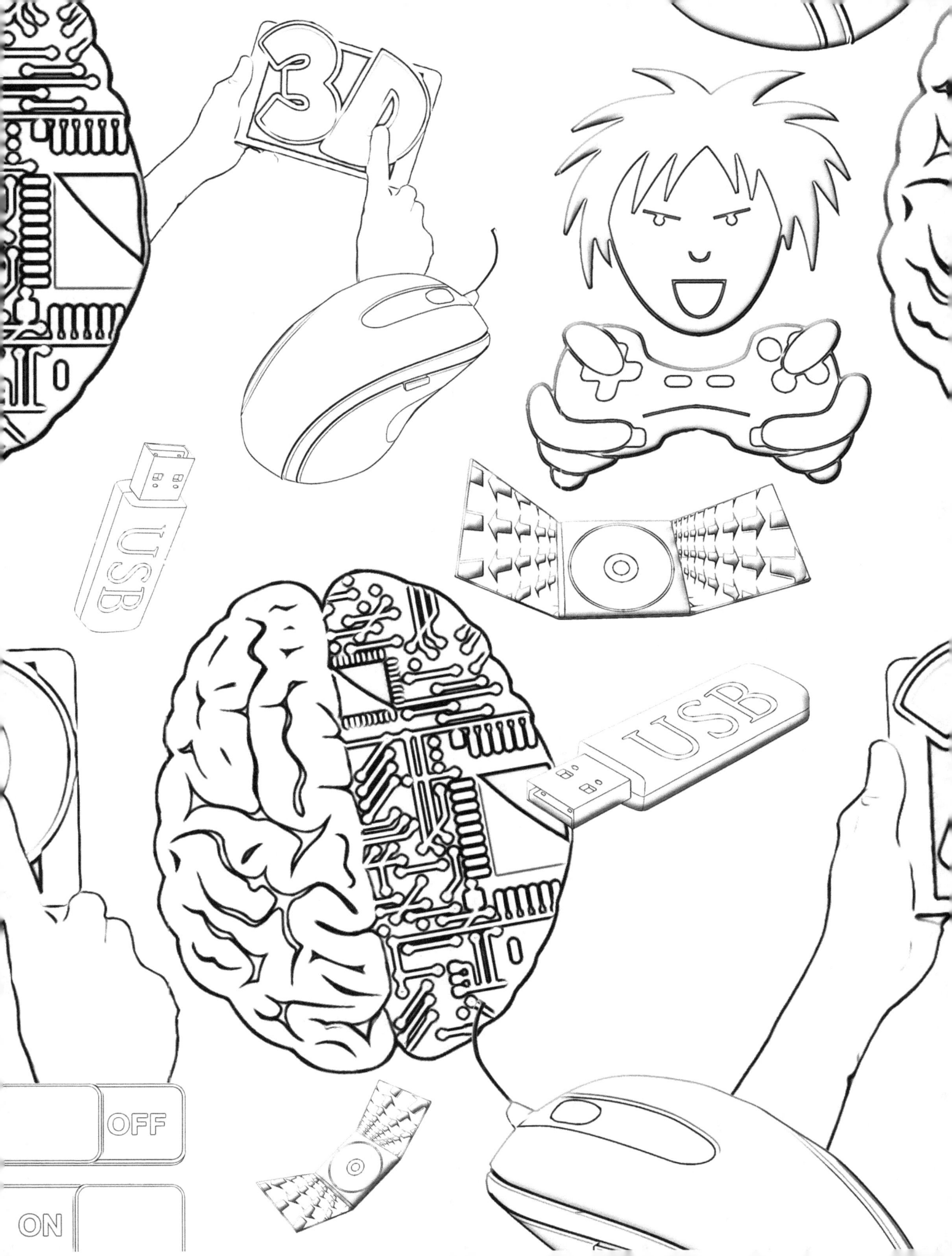

Also By Vibrant Books:

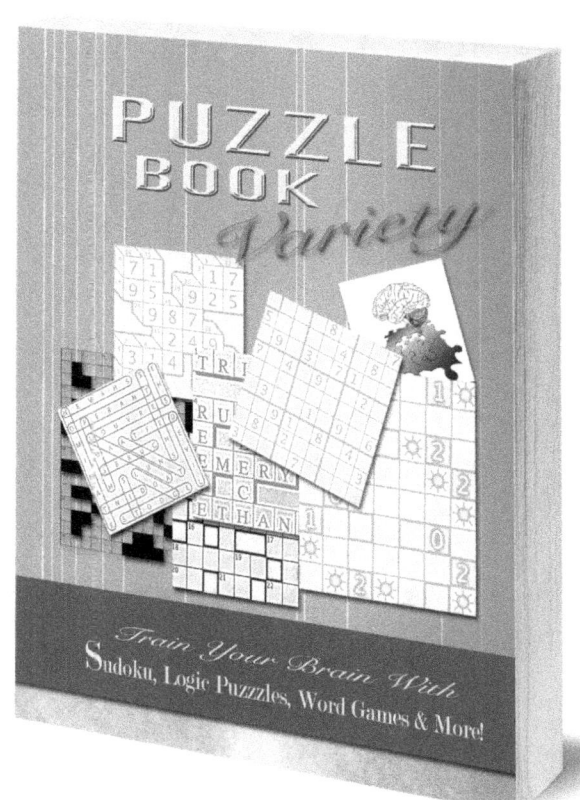

200 PUZZLES

Train your Brain With Sudoku, Logic Puzzles, Word Games & More! Level: Medium to Medium Hard

Available at most bookstores on and offline. And on our website at www.

www.vibrant-puzzle-books.com
Join us @
 Facebook: VibrantBooks
Twitter: BooksVibrant
Pinterest: Vibrant_Books
Instagram: adult_coloring_puzzle_books